SOCIETY   Webb Memorial Trust

Fighting Poverty and Inequality in an Age of Affluence

Beatrice Webb's 1909 Minority Report to the Poor Law Commission first set out the vision, arguments and values of social justice that were to become the foundations of the modern welfare state. It challenged the dominant assumption that the poor were solely to blame for their own poverty, demonstrating that the causes of poverty are structural as well as individual, and argued that society has a collective responsibility to prevent poverty, not merely alleviate it.

Culminating in 2009, Fighting poverty and inequality in an age of affluence will commemorate the centenary of the Minority Report by making a major contemporary contribution to the strategy for fighting poverty and inequality in today's Britain.

At a time when arguments about the causes of poverty, the principles of social justice and the responsibilities of the state are again central and contested issues in our political discourse, the project will explore how the Minority Report's key insights should be renewed and applied today. In doing so, the project will set out some core principles of contemporary citizenship that should underpin a new welfare settlement for the 21st century, as well as a series of practical proposals that will make a real difference to tackling poverty and inequality.

For further information about the project's research programme, events and publications, please visit the Fabian Society's web site at: www.fabians.org.uk/research/fightingpoverty.

Fabian Society
11 Dartmouth Street
London SW1H 9BN
www.fabians.org.uk

Fabian Policy Report 62
Editorial Director: Tom Hampson
Editorial Manager: Ed Wallis

First published 2009

ISBN 978 0 7163 3062 2

We would especially like to thank:

Webb Memorial Trust

British Library Cataloguing in Publication data.
A catalogue record for this book is available from the British Library.

Printed and bound by DG3

In the Mix

Narrowing the gap between public and private housing

James Gregory

Acknowledgements

Nick Raynsford and Daniel Zeichner, in particular, are owed special thanks, by both me and the Fabian Society. Nick and Daniel have done a huge amount for the Society's Housing Network, dedicating much of their time and effort to speak at our events. They have also given indispensible advice and guidance on the content and argument of this Report.

There has also been a wide range of input from the many individuals and organisations that have attended our policy seminars or who have been generous enough to spare their time for one to one interviews. Much of that input has directly contributed to this Policy Report. Hyde Plus, of Hyde Housing, and Notting Hill Housing have been especially helpful in this regard.

I would also like to thank the Fabian staff, especially Tom Hampson, Tim Horton, and Rosie Clayton.

Contents

A timeline of British social housing

1946 Bevan makes his 'living tapestry' speech to the House of Commons. The first generation of post-war council house babies are born – a generation which prospered throughout their lives.

1947 Conservatives in opposition call for a 'property owning democracy' at annual conference.

1951 The rush to volume. Conservatives elected on the promise to build 300,000 new homes per annum.

1955 Conservative Party's second post-war term.

1956 Building subsidies restricted to special needs housing – such as slum clearances and housing for the elderly.

1965 Labour White Paper, *Housing Programme*: the expansion of public housing only to meet 'exceptional need'. A new political consensus on the targeting of public housing.

1970 The 1970 cohort born. The first generation of council house babies to grow up being disadvantaged by where they live.

1977 Housing (Homeless Persons) Act. Local Authorities have a duty to house the homeless.

1980 The right to buy. The property owning democracy goes live.

2005 **To date,** 1.7 million homes sold under the right to buy.

2009 1.8 million households on the waiting list for public housing.

Summary
Apartheid cities

Britain is not broken and public housing is not all about 'sink estates'. Nevertheless, while most of our public housing serves its tenants very well, the evidence that this report presents strongly suggests that concentrated public housing is not just a symptom of poverty and disadvantage but is also a cause.

For many people, our housing policy has been nothing short of disastrous. By the age of 30, public housing tenants born in 1970 are twice as likely as the population as a whole to suffer from mental health problems, eleven times more likely to be not in employment education or training, and nine more likely to live in a workless household.

But this is not only about the poor. As many middle class homeowners, first time buyers, and people living in cities know, housing policy has failed across many social groups. And this is only being made worse by the recession.

We need to get housing right for the recession years and for the longer term. This report finds a strong association between public housing and worklessness. Given the lack of support provided by our benefits system this also means that there are very high levels of income poverty too.

Public housing is tainted by association with the imagery and stigma of the sink estate and this undermines popular support for all public housing. The mutual respect we owe each other becomes undermined, with some citizens seen as welfare dependents and somehow 'other':

alien beings in a subculture that horrifies and fascinates middle England in equal measure. This report makes hard policy proposals to deal with our 'apartheid cities'.

The repercussions of this 'othering' corrode the moral and political legitimacy of the welfare state, making it harder to justify the redistribution of wealth and resources that is needed if public housing is to be valued as a vital public good like the NHS.

How to narrow the gap

Breaking this vicious circle requires a fundamental shift in the way we think about public housing and simply building more houses cannot be the answer. The 1970s 'rush to volume' was a mistake then and it would be now. Instead we need a series of reforms that rebalance our housing to meet our needs.

- **Mix public and private housing**

  We need to pursue housing mix with real conviction. This means integrating public housing with private housing, not just in special project 'mixed communities', but across the full range of our housing stock. Though this kind of mix is currently considered best practice in planning guidelines, it is too often only honoured in the breech.

- **Use housing management holistically**

  Public housing management needs to be about far more than maintenance and rent collection. It should also be used as a means of delivering employment and training services, through the use of proactive outreach programmes where necessary.

- **Replace Housing Benefit with a Housing Cost Credit**

  This report suggests an outline for a Housing Cost Credit (HCC) to replace not only Housing Benefit, but all forms of financial assistance that the state provides to meet housing need. Crucially, this will include all the current (and future) measures to assist homeowners experiencing difficulty in servicing their mortgage payments.

■ **Reassess the 'right to buy' and the 'right to sell'**
On the 'right to buy', we should admit that Labour in the 1980s was wrong about the benefits of the individual freedom it gave people. But the Tories got it disastrously wrong by failing to plan for the reduction in the housing stock it created. It also led to the increasing concentration of poverty in the public housing that remains. A right to buy a home should not mean that tenants should have a right to take public housing stock with them if and when they choose to leave the tenure.

So we need a rebalancing: a remodelled and reassessed right to buy with a right to sell. Labour should introduce a flexible option to sell, in which households are given the option of transferring some or all of their equity to their Local Authority, thereby reducing mortgage payments to a manageable level.

In the Mix

Introduction
Nick Raynsford MP

Social housing is now – probably more that at any time in its 120 year history – the focus for controversy. Over the first 80 to 90 years of that period it was seen overwhelmingly as part of the solution (indeed sometimes the only solution) to this country's housing problems. There was widespread confidence that the provision of more social housing, predominantly but not exclusively built and managed by local councils, was the right way forward.

Over the past 30 to 40 years however, a growing number of voices have questioned whether social housing hasn't itself become part of the problem. The number of new social homes being built during this period has been way below the levels constructed in the immediate post-war era, and the sale of council housing under the right to buy has significantly diminished the stock. So social housing, provided by councils and housing associations combined, now represents only one fifth of the country's housing stock compared with one third that were owned by councils alone just 30 years ago. This decline is not universally seen as unfortunate. On the contrary some commentators have even proposed an end to the provision of social rented housing altogether.

Paradoxically, the level of demand for social housing remains very high. In the midst of the most severe downturn in the housing market for decades, the number of people applying to go on council waiting lists has risen dramatically.

So how do we explain this conundrum of large scale demand, but growing doubts about the appropriateness of the response? The answer lies partly in the changed nature of the social housing tenure, and the characteristics of those living in social housing, and partly in the wider economic and social environment in which it is now operating.

Put crudely, social housing represented an aspiration for a substantial proportion of the population for its first 70 to 80 years. It offered higher quality accommodation than most available alternatives and tenants were selected in such a way that many of the poorest and most disadvantaged were excluded.

Over the past 40 years or so, this has changed fundamentally. Social housing is now widely perceived as a 'residual' sector that houses only those who are unable to afford what are seen as more attractive alternatives and hence disproportionately accommodating those without work or with a range of disadvantages. At the same time the shortage of affordable accommodation, exacerbated by steep increases in house prices and a persistent undersupply of new homes, means that social housing remains the only viable option for larger numbers of people. But only a relatively small proportion of those on waiting lists get housed. While allocation policies continue, understandably, to give priority to those in greater need, the concentration of the poor and disadvantaged in social housing is inevitably perpetuated and social mix becomes ever harder to achieve. All of this reinforces the process of social separation and stigmatisation of social housing.

These are of course generalisations and as such inevitably oversimplify the much more complex reality in which most residents of social housing developments live. Indeed to a considerable extent the polarisation of opinion in the past 40 years about social housing has contributed to unhelpful caricatures and stereotypes of the tenure. Particularly with the benefit of substantial recent investment in the 'decent homes' programme and neighbourhood renewal, many council and housing association tenants feel great pride in their homes and the areas in which they live. They rightly deplore the stigmatizing processes associated with criticisms of the alleged failure of social housing.

Not only do these stereotypes misrepresent the more complex and richer patterns which exist in the real world, they also contribute to two misguided and dangerous policy responses. On the one hand there are those who advocate the end of security of tenure for social housing, seeing it as a transitory tenure to help people through adversity, but not as a basis for long-term occupancy. Take away security of tenure, they say, and this will free up many more tenancies that can be let to people in immediate need – a housing equivalent of the 'bed blocking' analysis of the situation affecting hospital beds in the NHS.

What those who advocate this approach fail to recognise is that it will simply intensify the 'problem' which they see with social housing – an exclusive concentration of unemployed and disadvantaged people locked in dependency. What chance is there of creating a better social mix, let alone a community spirit and a sense of commitment to the area, if the reward for anyone getting a job or a better income is the receipt of a notice to quit? "Time to move on to make way for someone in greater need" is a recipe for perpetual residualisation of the estate. Ironically the advocates of this policy would be the first to object if their entitlement to occupy a home of their own were to be arbitrarily threatened by some higher authority. "An Englishman's home is his castle" is the policy they apply to themselves, but wish to deny to their less fortunate fellow citizens.

But equally misguided is the belief that the way forward is the resumption of large scale council home building programmes. Yes, we do need an expanded supply of social and affordable housing and indeed of other housing tenures, but these should not be built in mono-tenure estates. One of the curious characteristics of 20th century housing policy was the adoption of what can only be described as social apartheid. In the 30 years that followed the end of the second world war, we saw the largest scale housebuilding programme in the country's history. Politicians promised to build ever more homes – and they delivered. Harold Macmillan built 300,000 new homes a year in the 1950s; Harold Wilson built 400,000 homes a year in the 1960s.

These new homes were almost exclusively owner-occupied or council, but they rarely if ever were built together. Each had their own separate location, as if it were unthinkable for people of different tenure to live next door to each other. Yet that has been the norm for most of the 5000 or so years of recorded world history. Not only did people of different economic and social status live in the same street or village in medieval England, they often lived in the same home, with a few animals as well thrown in for good measure! These patterns persisted until the 19th century. Of course wealthier people enjoyed much grander and more comfortable accommodation than others, and within the home 'upstairs' and 'downstairs' were clearly delineated. But the rule that people of different economic status should live in entirely separate geographical areas did not become the norm until the mass housing programmes of the mid 20th century.

And a very unhappy change of policy it has proved. While council housing remained an aspiration for large sections of the better-off working class, the disastrous consequences of this social apartheid were not fully felt. But once council housing became a residual sector accommodating a disproportionate number of the poorest and most disadvantaged members of society, the dire results of this social separation came home to roost.

That is why the return to mixed tenure communities is such a crucial issue, and why this Fabian pamphlet fulfils such a valuable role in the debate about the future of housing policy. Unlike too many other recent contributions from think tanks which show little or no appreciation of the real-world realities, this publication offers a thoughtful and thorough analysis of the problem of residualisation and social segregation, and the damaging impact this has on people's life chances. James Gregory also recognises that the problem goes far wider than simply housing policy. Solutions depend on a range of well-integrated responses, addressing education, health, employment, crime and other issues as well as housing.

To an extent we have begun to learn this lesson. The fact that the responsible government department is now known as Communities and Local Government, rather than Housing and Local Government as it was in the immediate post-war era, is an indication of the change in thinking. Housing and planning policy has championed the cause of mixed tenure and balanced communities for more than a decade. And even among the housebuilders, who for most of the 20th century were intransigent about the need to segregate owner-occupation from social housing to retain its value (the infamous Cutteslowe Walls referred to on page 19 of this pamphlet providing a characteristic example), there is growing recognition that well designed mixed tenure developments can succeed socially, economically and environmentally.

In the current recession, funding from the Homes and Communities Agency for social and affordable housing as part of mixed tenure developments is likely to prove a highly attractive proposition to the home-building industry. Our challenge is to ensure that this commitment doesn't evaporate when recovery comes. But even more challenging, as this pamphlet recognises, will be the task of turning round existing mono-tenure estates which suffer from stigmatisation and social segregation. There are good examples of success which demonstrate the scope for transformational change even in very deprived areas. Sensible housing allocations policies which do not reinforce concentrations of unemployed and disadvantaged people in one area have a role to play.

So too does good management and maintenance. Too many 'sink' estates started life as model developments but have been allowed to deteriorate. Hence the tendency of older, long established tenants of council housing estates to reminisce nostalgically about how lovely the place was when they first moved in, often contrasting this very unfavourably with its current state. Once the rot sets in and estates get a bad name, the task of returning them to normality is much harder. So active management and prompt and efficient maintenance services have a key role to play.

However, the overwhelming evidence is that the turnaround of a problem estate cannot be accomplished by housing policies alone. When there is widespread worklessness and unemployment, active intervention to assist people to acquire the skills and confidence necessary to secure lasting employment will be vital. Similarly measures to tackle problems of crime, drug abuse and anti-social behaviour may be essential, as well as new opportunities and facilities for youngsters who in the past had too few chances for constructive play or leisure activity. The good news is that an increasing number of more progressive councils and housing associations are recognising the need for comprehensive approaches that incorporate a range of different elements to break down the sense of social separation and isolation that can affect some stigmatised estates.

Building on the perceptive and thorough analysis of the problems this pamphlet concludes with a series of recommendations on actions which can help achieve the objective of normalising areas which have become stigmatised and isolated from the mainstream of society. As with any comprehensive set of recommendations some are more likely to succeed than others, but in the best Fabian tradition this pamphlet sets a clear direction based on a sound evidence base and invites us to respond. There can be few more important political challenges in the coming years and 'In the Mix' deserves the closest attention from those responsible for defining the policies on which a Labour government should fight the forthcoming election.

1 | Public housing and life chances

New Labour's promise

Shortly after coming to power in 1997, Tony Blair paid a now-famous visit to the Aylesbury Estate in south London, chosen as the location for his first speech as Prime Minister. In the language of inclusion that was to set the tone of the New Labour project, Blair declared that there would be an end to "no go areas": there would be no areas in which the poor and marginalised could simply be parked and forgotten by the affluent majority.

Almost immediately, the newly created Social Exclusion Unit pledged to close the gap between the poorest areas and their more prosperous neighbours. Then, in 2001 they produced the Neighbourhood Renewal Strategy, which has at its heart a core vision: that within ten to twenty years no one should be seriously disadvantaged by where they live.

Within policy circles an old, powerful ideal soon re-emerged: the 1945 ideal of Labour minister Nye Bevan that "the doctor, the grocer, the butcher and the farm labourer all lived in the same street".[1] Today, Bevan's aspiration towards the "living tapestry of the mixed community" is expressed in the rather more prosaic Planning Policy Statement 3: "To create sustainable, inclusive, mixed communities in all areas, both urban and rural".[2]

Yet, despite real effort over the last decade to make good on these aspirations, and some important successes, from regeneration projects to improvement in the quality of public housing stock, no-one could seriously argue that people are not still disadvantaged – often acutely so – by where they live. And as for Bevan's noble aspiration, many people on the British left now feel that the historic failure of successive governments – including the current Government – to fulfil this is profound. They see a failure in housing policy that has achieved the exact opposite of mix – the segregation of so much public housing, resulting in concentrated pockets of poverty, and the very great social polarisation that our rising general affluence has left in its wake. The consequence has not only been the continuation of a strong connection between public housing, place and poverty, but a set of processes that actually foster and entrench the poverty of social tenants.

This pamphlet explores the residualisation of public housing and the segregation it has generated, why it impacts adversely on the life chances of those who use public housing, and what can be done about it. Chapter 2 provides a brief history of public housing, exploring how we got into this position and, from a historical perspective, which policy approaches can be said to have succeeded or failed. Chapter 3 offers a theoretical model of how residualisation can foster and exacerbate poverty and exclusion, and illustrates how this has worked in the case of public housing. Finally, building on this historical and theoretical analysis, Chapter 4 looks at some possible policy solutions for tackling the residualisation of public housing and improving the life chances of those who use it.

Some facts about housing, place and poverty

The area you live in – your neighbourhood – can have an effect on how disadvantaged you are. Statistical analysis of the British Household Panel Survey has shown that, over the life-cycle, an individual's chances of gaining employment or leaving poverty were significantly reduced if he or she lived in a poor area, a finding that is backed up by international evidence from a range of countries.[3,4] Take two individuals with the same skills, qualifications, and health, place them in neighbourhoods with different levels of poverty or affluence, and the life chances of one are likely to be significantly worse than for the other.

For those who like their facts to come with drama and colour, the evidence on the link between poverty, place and physical health outcomes is even more striking. A recent World Health Organisation report provides us with a truly schocking fact: in Calton in Glasgow, average male life expectancy is a pathetic 54 years.[5]

Beyond these neighbourhood effects, however, the tenure of public housing itself is strongly correlated with a wide range of social disadvantage. In particular, the analysis of individuals born in 1970 demonstrates the following (strong) correlations. Being in public housing at the age of 30 meant that, compared to the population as a whole, you were: twice as likely to suffer from mental health problems (such as anxiety and depression) and to have a low sense of 'self-efficacy'; eleven times more likely to be not in employment, education, or training; and nine more likely to live in a workless household.[6]

A broad range of social disadvantage associated with being in public housing at the age of 30, for the 1970 cohort, is illustrated in Figure 1.

In his review of the future of public housing, the respected social policy academic John Hills came to a similar conclusion regarding worklessness: "even controlling for a very wide range of personal characteristics, the likelihood of someone in public housing being employed appears significantly lower in than those in other tenures".[7]

Beyond this, robust academic research has demonstrated a strong correlation between housing tenure and mental health problems, with public housing tenants more likely than others to be affected.[8] And there are important neighbourhood effects here too: those living in electoral wards with concentrated unemployment are more likely to suffer from depression and anxiety once they have been affected by physical ill-health, and are less likely to recover in a reasonable time frame after the onset of these psychological conditions.[9]

Such correlations, of course, are partly a product of the allocation system. The chronic undersupply of public housing, coupled with a needs-based allocation system, means that public housing is now what

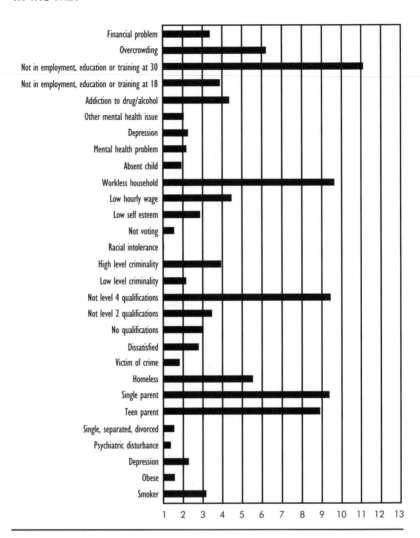

Figure 1 Social housing tenure in 2000 and multiple disadvantage, 1970 cohort. Odds ratios for co-occurrence of social exclusion outcomes with social housing tenure, age 30.

An odds ratio of two means, for example, that 30-year olds in social housing had odds twice as high of having this characteristic as those of the general population, for example 1/5 instead of 1/10.

might be called a 'poverty tenure' because only the poorest people are filtered into it. So here tenure is a symptom rather than a cause.

But even taking this into account, the emerging statistical evidence confirms what a stream of anecdotal evidence over several decades has continuously suggested: in certain contexts, public housing can itself be part of the causal processes of poverty.

A recent longitudinal study, based on four major birth cohort data sets that stretch back to 1946, has found that, even once we control for a whole range of individual and family background variables, both housing tenure and area matter for later life outcomes.[10]

For those born in 1946, growing up in public housing was not associated with increased risk of disadvantage later in life. Yet for the cohort born in 1970, the impact of tenure on life chances was profound. For this latter group, growing up in public housing was associated with a significantly increased risk of disadvantage later in life (such as worklessness, financial problems, and depression). Similar associations between social housing tenure in early adultholld and disadvantage in later adulthood were also found.

Significantly, these effects remained even when controlling for a range of background variables which might otherwise explain the correlation of housing tenure and adult deprevation (variables such as education, family income, and occupation), suggesting such statistical associations are due to the impact of housing tenure rather than to the factors that lead individuals to be in public housing in the first place.[11] And only some of the link between tenure and subsequent disadvantage can be accounted for by area effects.

What accounted for this change in the life chances of social tenants between the 1946 and 1970 cohorts? This pamphlet argues that a key element was a change in the nature of public housing in this period, and presents a histoical and institutional analysis of this change, along with an examination of some of the causal mechanisms that underlie this connection between tenure and life chances. But one conclusion should jump out from the very start: there is nothing inevitable about this correlation

11

between housing and disadvantage. It has been caused by political and institutional processes – and such processes can be arrested and altered.

The residualisation of public housing

The most important of these processes, and the central theme of this pamphlet, is the *residualisation* of public housing since 1946. Residualisation means two things, both of which are central to the argument of this pamphlet.

- **Public housing for the poor only**
  Firstly, residualisation is what happens when public housing becomes highly targeted, aimed at an ever-smaller group labelled as 'the poor'.
- **Geographically concentrated public housing**
  The second process follows, as we shall see, from the first. As well as public housing being targeted only a certain class of individual, it is also increasingly geographically concentrated, as we have seen with the huge monolithic estates of the 1960s.

The net result of these processes has been the increasing polarisation of public housing, physically isolated and socially marginalised from mainstream housing provision.

The statistics bear this out. The number of individuals living in social housing in England has declined dramatically from 42 per cent of the population in 1979 to just over 19 per cent in 2002. While in 1979 over forty per cent of social housing tenants were in the top half of the income distribution, today this figure has more than halved.[12]

One key driver of this trend has been the increase in home ownership over the same period among middle- and higher-income households. Between 1965 and 2003, the proportion of the most disadvantaged 40 per cent owning their own homes fell, while that amongst the remaining 60 per cent rose; for those in the middle quintile, the proportion of owners rose from 34 per cent to 64 per cent.[13] And with the dramatic increase in housing value over this time, the result has not only been a polarisation of the population in terms of tenure, but also in terms of wealth.

Added to this there is the literal spatial segregation and concentration of public housing that has always been a feature of housing in Britain, but which was greatly accelerated in the 1970s and 1980s. The clearest expression of this aspect of residualisation is, of course, to be found in the relatively small – but tremendously symbolic – proportion of public housing that is concentrated on large estates. It is in these estates that the two processes of residualisation come together in a double whammy against fair life-chances: council housing given only to the poorest, and the poorest thereby corralled into deprived neighbourhoods.

So the location of Blair's 1997 Aylesbury Estate speech was well chosen. Not only did the estate exemplify the processes of residualisation and disadvantage I have just sketched, but the visual profile and image of the estate also captured the immensely powerful symbolism that the imagery of the 'sink-estate' still evokes. It is a symbolism that part reflects and part creates the realities of life in the most deprived neighbourhoods – always areas with very high concentrations of social housing, and invariably associated in the public imagination with the housing of the monolithic 'council' estate that is now very often - in the world of ALMOs and Large Scale Voluntary Transfers - no longer a council estate at all.

The literal, spatial concentration of such estates clearly tells a story about the polarisation of different types of housing across the UK. And as well as a concentration of tenure, there has been a concentration of income too.[14] As Danny Dorling has observed, this polarisation has brought with it a process of social distancing: "Poor, rich and average households became less and less likely to live next door to one another between 1970 and 2000".[15] In particular, since the 1980s, there has been increasing clustering and concentration of the 'breadline poor' (those on the cusp, moving in and out of poverty), who are increasingly spatially separated from both average and wealthy households.[16]

It is significant that this is not just a story of the poor being pushed to one side: the wealthy are also exiting, often walling themselves away in urban gated communities. It is not just, it seems, that the aspiration in Britain is to own rather than to rent quality social housing – it is also to place as much distance as possible between the 'independent' affluent and the stigmatised poor in social housing. If those in the middle – the 'average' households do not themselves manage to attain such distance, we should nevertheless be in no doubt about the spirit of the aspiration; an aspiration that the ideology of right to buy tapped into perhaps, but also did so much to create and nurture.

These processes of residualisation have also led to the segregation of many people from the rest of society. We have seen public housing tenants differentiated from the majority of citizens, often with less access to sources of wealth generation, jobs, services, social networks and so on. These are all things which have an adverse impact on people's life chances.

We must be measured in our discussion of the broader context, though. One of the central conclusions of John Hills' landmark report on social housing is that the great majority of public housing does precisely what it is meant to do: it provides stable, quality housing for those in need who can't afford to access this basic good in the private market. Hills points out that, "Consideration of the future role of social housing does not take place against the background of a general crisis in housing conditions – if anything, the reverse. But that general improvement means that the wide variations in conditions between households should remove any sense of complacency".[17] And there is a crucial point that Hills acknowledges but does not build on: the sense in which the pathological cases of public housing failure not only fail to serve those in housing need, but also undermine broader public support for a robust welfare settlement that treats all citizens with the respect and dignity that they deserve.

Despite all this, though, the sad fact is that public housing, while often being part of the solution to tackling poverty and inequality can also sometimes be part of the problem. At best, it has failed to overcome the disadvantage and exclusion suffered by many tenants; at worst, it has been an active cause of them.

2 | Why mixing has failed so far

Where you live definitely has an impact on your life chances. As discussed in Chapter 1, those born in 1970 who grew up in public housing were more likely to be disadvantaged later in life than those not in public housing – a link that did not exist in 1946. While the academic analysis is wary of talking about causes here, there is a compelling historical story to be told about the decline of the status and value of public housing, which points to a number of possible causes for this connection between public housing tenure and disadvantage. It is the story of residualisation.

Two political events are of particular significance in this story. The first is the 1977 Housing (Homeless Persons) Act, which placed on Local Authorities the statutory duty to house the homeless. The second is the 1980 Housing Act, which introduced the landmark 'right to buy' legislation, giving council housing tenants the right to buy their rented home.

The first of these Acts helped residualise the public housing system by increasing the numbers of the most disadvantaged households who were filtered into social housing (which we will call 'inflow'); and the second, over time, led to the loss (or 'outflow') of the most independent and least disadvantaged households from the neighbourhoods that they had once rented in as council tenants.

At the same time, there was a dramatic reduction in the supply of new public housing: combined council and Housing Association completions totalled approximately 130, 000 new units in 1975, but this had fallen to 94, 000 units in 1980. Moreover, the trend was to continue: by 1990 the total number of social housing completions in that year had fallen to just under 28,000.[18]

The net result was the further concentration of poverty and disadvantage: less housing available, with the remaining stock being targeted at those most in need.

But these residualising processes were by no means new. A history of social housing in Britain quickly reveals that, although the 1977 and 1980 Housing Acts were important turning points, there are deep continuities in these processes which stretch far further back.

Housing for the working classes and the needy

In 1893 the London County Council began building the Boundary Street Estate on the site of the Old Nichol slum. The aim was housing for the 'working classes', but specifically the 'respectable working classes'. And so, from the very start, an institutional filtering mechanism was embedded in the provision of public housing. That mechanism for judging respectability was rent – high rent.

The motivation was not in fact entirely dissimilar to recent government pronouncements linking tenancy to employment aspiration: these estates were to be working estates. But the practical upshot was that only the artisan classes could afford to live on the Boundary Estate. The great majority of residents from the Old Nichol were pushed elsewhere, and the Boundary became populated largely by affluent artisans. Those that did not meet the criterion of respectability were left to rely on the cheapest end of the private rented sector, and it was this sector that remained the slum dwelling all the way up to the 1970s.[19] Public housing in the modern era, it seems, started as it meant to go on: selection and classification – the filtering of different 'types' of respectable and unrespectable tenants – into different types of housing.

Indeed, in many respects, the history of public housing *is* just the history of allocations; of who lives in it, where and why – and particularly, as we have just seen, who gets to live in the most attractive public housing.

Originally, then, housing for the 'working classes' did not automatically carry negative connotations. On the contrary, it marked residents off from those that were merely 'needy' – and to be needy was to be just a stone's throw away from 'undeserving'. And if the new estates built after the First World War marked the physical manifestation of this categorisation of people into 'types', then so much the better: it would simplify the practical policy responses to a social analysis driven by the categories, and would fit neatly into the mentality of rewards and status that came with the powerful ideological legacy of Poor Law thinking.

The more respectable connotations of public housing began to change in the period between the wars, however, as governments put increasing emphasis on subsidies that were tied to slum clearances – a change that the social housing experts Power and Houghton describe as a "narrowing of purpose" which culminated in the abolition in 1933 of general subsidies for housing that was not built specifically to tackle overcrowding and slum conditions.[20] While, at first sight, this seems to be a just development – the targeting of resources where they were truly needed – it became an early driver of the residualisation of public housing and a change in its public image. When public subsidy became explicitly attached to the label of 'slum clearance', it should come as no surprise that it increasingly bore the marks of stigma.

Social distance and segregation

An extraordinary story exemplifies the power of this separation, a simple snobbery that exerted the most pernicious influence when backed by official and legal sanction. When the Cutteslowe council estate was built in North Oxford in 1933, there was every reason to think that the estate could and would provide the best that social housing could offer: quality homes built in a desirable part of Oxford, two miles from the city centre. Indeed, so desirable was the land that a private developer immediately bought an a prime plot next to it, built a number of desirable homes for private sale; and promptly built two nine foot walls (with revolving spikes on top), directly blocking the road that led from the council estate to the private dwellings. As a direct result of these walls, the Cutteslowe residents no longer had direct access to the shops and busses that had serviced the estate, and had to make a diversion of over a mile instead. Perhaps the most extraordinary feature of the story is that the fact the walls remained all the way up until 1959; and in the face of continuous protest and council action, and even a Bill in Parliament.[21]

But the attitudes and beliefs that this story represents was by no means unique. The developer built the walls because he believed that proximity to council housing undermined the value of the private estate. The aspiration of those buying the private homes was already being shaped, across the country, by the desire for social and physical distance from social housing. When building societies in the 1930s brought homeownership into the reach of the more affluent, skilled working classes, the stigma of the 'council estate' had already taken hold. This was, inevitably, reflected in the attitudes of developers, even where the reaction was not as extreme as the Cutteslowe episode. "As far as possible private estates signified social distance from both council housing and inner terraces, with mock Tudor gables, smart porches, front gardens and paired semis, not rows".[22]

And the Cutteslowe story is not unique precisely because there was a systemic, institutional process driving the aspirational desire for social distance. The Cutteslowe estate had been built as part of Oxford's slum clearance programme, and no matter how well located or designed, this concentration of poverty left an indelible social imprint on the estate: that it only for the poor.

The resulting social concentration and segregation was thus the fundamental failing of interwar social housing in Britain. This lesson was nailed down with precision when, after the first half century of social housing, and just after the second of the two world wars, the town planner Thomas Sharp published his book, *Town Planning*. In it, he warned of:

> "social concentration camps: places in which one social class is concentrated to the exclusion of all others...around the great cities we have enormous one-class communities (if they can be called communities) the like of which the world has never seen before; Becontree, where no less than 120,000 work-class people live in one enormous concentration: Norris Green, one of many Liverpool Corporation Estates, housing 50,000 working-class inhabitants".[23]

Sharp had two key messages. The first was the simple moral principle that these estates represented an acute form of social apartheid, something more than simple snobbery that even approached ethnic segregation, as if the poor were a separate species to be hived off into concentration camps.

Sharp's second message is less normative and more practical, and contains the key insight that poorly planned social housing is not just a misfortune that the poor must suffer, but also a powerful cause of poverty. The concentration camps that he refers to are clearly isolated, and marked off from mainstream society. But they were very frequently isolated from both public services and, crucially, labour markets. Ironically, Cutteslowe was actually one of the more blessed estates; built in the city, rather than pushed to the hinterlands, and well connected to the thriving labour market of the growing car industry.

Yet even when well connected to transport and labour markets, we also have another historical lesson that was perhaps not so easily available to Sharp. This is the lesson of Chapter 1 of this essay: concentrations of poverty and worklessness create cultural norms and social expectations that themselves become not just symptoms of poverty, but powerful causes as well. Even where the physical distances to labour markets are small, the sheer concentration of poverty itself has a constraining effect, barring individuals from accessing the opportunities that, to the external observer, are apparently so near.

In these ways, then, mass public housing was becoming one of the structural causes of poverty; and so the 'deserving' poor – the working poor – often came to be workless. A leg up into public housing in fact became a kick in the teeth: not more respect and respectability, but a descent into the class of the undeserving poor.

The corrective was to be the ideal of mixed communities – neighbourhoods with a social mix and balance – a wide range of incomes and household types representing a cross section of society more broadly. The ideal also encompasses something broader – that the balance across the full range of housing stock across can help create a more mixed, integrated society. The deep point of principle, of course, remains the same: housing should not be a vehicle for the creation of social ghettoes or part of the processes of social exclusion. At present, it is very clearly part of this story.

The new Jerusalem

In 1939 three quarters of new homes were still built for the private sector. This balance was to be turned on its head in the years following the war. Bevan saw public housing as one of the key institutions of the new welfare state. But this was not only the solution to the 'Squalor' that Beveridge identified as one of the 'five giants' to be slain. Nor was this just a race to volume. It was not good enough simply to lift the poor out of squalor. There was a deeper moral vision too: the ideals of equality and mix.

Bevan's vision can be summed up in his two most famous quotes. The first seemingly related just to design: "We shall be judged for a year or two by the number of houses that we build. We shall be judged in ten years time by the type of houses we build". But it is in the second that we get the flavour of the moral vision: social housing was to be part of "the living tapestry of a mixed community" where "the doctor, the grocer, the butcher and the farm labourer all lived in the same street". The two statements are, in fact, intimately linked by the ideal of equality. What's good enough for the doctor is good enough for the labourer: there was to be no visible or moral distinction between types of person or tenure. Indeed, Bevan forced through a potentially radical legislative and categorical change. Running directly counter to the long history of sociological classification of 'the poor', Bevan in 1948 Bevan removed the pre-war legislative requirement that social housing was only to be provided for the 'working classes'. To provide social housing just for the working classes was, for Bevan, to perpetuate a hierarchy of snobbery, and to present future planners with the temptation to build to inferior standards; thus providing, once again, a physical manifestation of social distinctions.

The ideal of mix was no empty dream either: it was a central plank of the Labour Government's vision of a new welfare society. It was to be the planning philosophy underpinning the 1946 New Towns Act, for example. Finally numbering twenty eight in total, these new towns eventually housed some two million people. They came in three phases, with towns such as Stevenage and Hatfield in the first phase, and – perhaps the most well known of all – Milton Keynes only being built in a third phase in the 1960s. Key lessons had been learnt from the errors of interwar planning, and many New Towns were largely successful, designed specifically to avoid the isolation and segregation of interwar public housing, even if the ideal of social mix was achieved only incompletely and partially.[24] Public housing was no longer an official vehicle of segregation. Even where it still performed this function in practice, the language of justification had to change: the moral presumption, at this particular point in history, was for mix.

The rush to volume – and race to the bottom

So what went wrong in the following decades? A full history of the decline and residualisation of public housing since the war would need to embrace many factors. Structural transformations in the economy shifted whole populations into worklessness; the rented sector was allowed to decline to such a degree that it became the host of a new series of slum dwellings; modernist utopian architecture seemed to almost build blight into the design of many estates; and a centralist governmental mentality rode roughshod over the wants and aspirations of tenants cleared out of the slums – perhaps not deserving of poverty but still, it would seem, not deserving of a public voice.

But it is the failure of Bevan's twin pillars of mix and quality that really stand out here. As Bevan saw so clearly, both in fact went hand in hand – in failure as well as in success. Despite all of his efforts to maintain the emphasis on quality over volume, this emphasis did not survive the transition to a Conservative government in 1951. Hugh Dalton, the Labour planning minister, himself had sanctioned a reduction in the standards of homes (against vociferous opposition from Bevan), and the Conservative Prime Minister Harold Macmillan then cut standards and space requirements still further in the rush to volume triggered by the hugely ambitious building targets the Conservatives had promised *en route* to power. So successful was this programme, in the mind of the Conservative elite, that subsidies for general housing were reduced in 1954. After 1956 building subsidies were restricted in scope too; being dedicated only to 'special' (highly targeted) projects such as the slum clearances and New Towns programme.[25]

The smaller homes were to be offered to the public as the 'people's house', available quickly and with lower rent. Very soon the house became a flat; available not just quickly, but almost literally off the shelf – the assembly line. 'System build', the system of the concrete tower blocks we are all so familiar with, came to be accepted as a cheap, quick way to furnish everyone with a place to live. It didn't take long for the positive role of the high rise to become an élite article of faith – among both the Conservatives and Labour. Financial incentives were put in place to encourage the private sector to build them, with in 1956 the Government introducing higher subsidies for blocks above fifteen storeys, which got three times the subsidy given to a house.

The results are revealed in the figures: in 1953 only three per cent of public sector housing new builds were in high-rise flats: by 1966 the figure had risen to twenty six per cent.[26,27] And, to add insult to injury, not only were these dwellings a social disaster, they were also expensive; an inefficient 'solution' that was part of the very problem it was designed to solve.

The spatial concentration generated by high-rise flats was reinforced by the way in which the continuing process of slum clearance was managed. The 1954 Housing Repairs and Rents Act retained the subsidy (from the 1930s) that was tied directly to the demolition and replacement of slum dwellings. As in the 1930s, those filtered into the new public housing were the residents of the cleared slums, and in the minds of many they were simply to take the stigma of the slum with them to their new home. The announcement that an area was to be part of the clearance program would almost immediately lead to an exodus of those with the means to do so, in part simply because of the stigma, but also because of the perception that the quality of the area (and the value of houses for those that owned) would very rapidly plummet.[28] In a process that would be almost exactly mirrored in the 1980s, those left behind were those least likely to be in stable work, and most likely to need the services of the welfare state. So the residents of these estates became labelled and categorised, and the estates were doomed to stigma - as well as very real concentrations of social need – from the start.

And when the time came to enter their new home, most residents would have found that both their social networks and their commercial services had either been lost, or very severely disrupted. Neighbours were split up by thoughtless allocation procedures and the level of commercial activity and opportunity was more than decimated. The Elthorne Estate in North Islington, for example, soon had only six shops compared with the ninety it had as a 'slum'.

There was also a wholesale destruction of precisely the type of housing stock that could have helped make the vision of mix a reality. In the aggressive clearances of the 1960s, a great deal of quality housing that only needed refurbishment was demolished; North Islington, for example, lost hundreds of attractive Georgian houses this way. Often all it took to condemn a home was shoddy plumbing or small windows. A 1967 Greater London Council survey found that a full sixty per cent of homes condemned to demolition were structurally sound.[29]

Behind the scenes, the official rationale for this – though not openly stated – was the need to clear more land for building new home; somewhat perversely, homes that would be needed precisely because the slum clearances and increased demand and swollen council waiting lists for housing.

This was planning failure on a vast scale. While mix was sought in the New Towns, it was systematically undermined by the construction of new monolithic estates, built to replace the communities that, with the right policies, offered the best hope of all for a genuine mix.

At the same time, the categorising of tenants into the 'deserving' and 'undeserving' continued unabated, all the way up into the 1970s and beyond. It was not just that public housing ceased to be mixed with other tenures; public housing itself was sub-divided into separate categories for different tenants. In the late 1970s, Tower Hamlets council (whose housing stock comprised of 80 per cent council housing), did nothing to hide the fact that it had an explicit policy of filtering all of its 'difficult' tenants into just one estate. Part of the motivation behind this was to prevent bad housing tenants dragging down good public housing areas. In this respect, the reaction was understandable: it sought to preserve the wider value of public housing. But there was also more than a whiff of that old distinction between the deserving and undeserving, the respectable and the unrespectable. And it was the stigma of the latter that was to stick in the popular imagination.

But there was also a more subtle process at work, one that is in fact intimately linked to the decline in the physical quality of housing under Macmillan and beyond. And this process lies in the history of the right to buy; a history of ideology – of a view of citizenship as independence – every bit as much as it is a history of housing and planning policy.

The property owning democracy

Bevan refused to compromise on the quality of public housing not just because he saw housing quality as a marker of social equality but also because he saw it as a long-term asset of the state and as the stable bedrock of communities. Tenants were to settle in their new homes; and thick, solidaristic communities would grow around them. Private ownership was not part of the vision. This was to change dramatically at the start of the Conservatives' second term of office in 1955. The new game in town was the goal of a "property owning democracy".

Anthony Eden, in opposition, had made the ideological call for ownership as early as the 1947 Conservative Party annual conference. In 1955 the vision started to be driven by structural changes in the housing economy, when the government moved to restore the traditional private-public balance. Private developers were to build for the aspirant property owning majority; councils were to build only for the rest. As it was assumed that the great majority should aspire to home ownership – if not immediately then in the near future – Bevan's emphasis on quality seemed, to Macmillan at least, to be misplaced. For these were to be temporary homes on the way towards a higher state of tenure; and, we should not forget, a greater respectability. Social housing tenure was temporary, and lower quality a short-term sacrifice that tenants could reasonably be expected to live with.

The electoral success of this housing strategy meant that Labour could not resist following it in the longer term. By 1965, Labour had fully converted to a mixed economy in housing supply. More ominously, a mixed economy brought with it a stark social distinction: private sector building for the aspirant owner; public sector building for those unable to live the dream. In Richard Crossman's 1965 White Paper this assumption is made particularly explicit: "The expansion of the public programme now proposed is to meet exceptional needs… the expansion of building for owner-occupation on the other hand is normal; it reflects a long-term social advance which should gradually pervade every region."[30] Thus, the Labour party had come round to the Conservative view of 1956: the public subsidy of housing was only to be for special projects and acute need. The new consensus thereby reverted to the old: public housing once again was to become welfare targeted only at the poor. And very quickly welfare for the poor became poor welfare – a residualised stock and services.[31]

Two turning points

The story so far is one of trends: a trend towards the residualisation of social housing, as the tenure of last resort targeted only on the needy; and a social and political trend that was captured by the rhetoric of the 'property owning democracy'. But, as I suggested at the start of this chapter, there are two crucial moments in which both these trends were crystallised in specific moments.

The first of these is the Callaghan Government's 1977 Housing (Homeless Persons) Act. Prior to this Act, there was no statutory obligation for Local Authorities to house the homeless. Those that were literally destitute were the responsibility not of the local housing department, but of the council's social services. Homeless families would be placed in so called Part III hostels that bore some striking resemblances to the workhouses of the Poor Law era; indeed, many *were* former workhouses. And the similarities did not stop there.[32] Typically, mothers and children were separated from fathers and placed in dormitory accommodation.

So the 1977 Act was a humane moment, apparently purging home-lessness of the last residues of Poor Law thinking, and putting an end to the shocking practices of the Part III hostels. But in retrospect the conclusion is unfortunately more qualified than this. For whilst the Act filtered more of the neediest households into public housing, no extra provision was made for housing supply, and an already rationed and targeted good became even more so. Without greater supply, public housing increasingly became the exclusive tenure of those with the greatest need, and a far cry from Bevan's ideal of mix. Certainly, there were still large numbers of more affluent working-class households in council housing, but these would now be much nearer the bottom of the queue if they had to reapply. Naturally enough, this process further cemented broader public perceptions of public housing as for the poorest – the type of 'dependent' person that the ideology of property owning democracy tacitly categorised as incomplete citizens.

The fullest fruition of this ideology was, of course, to come with the 1980 Housing Act, which brought in the landmark Right-to-Buy legisla-tion – the second key moment in underpinning the process of residual-isation. This imposed on Local Authorities the duty to sell to tenants who had been paying rent in their home, with discounts of up to 50 per cent of the market value, depending upon the length of their tenure. By 1989 discounts on council houses had become so steep that in some cases the discount was 70 per cent of market value.[33]

The right to buy soon proved enormously popular, and quickly became a central plank of the Thatcherite programme, and one of the most powerful unifying tools of the electoral coalition that saw that the traditional working classes shift their allegiance from Labour to Conservatives. So popular, in fact, that Labour soon abandoned its oppo-sition to the policy, and by 2005 1.7 million homes had been sold through the right to buy, under both Conservative and Labour administrations.

There were very good reasons for this popularity, and there were voices in the Labour Party that were calling for some version of the scheme in the late 1970s, before even Margaret Thatcher was a convert.

Labour's Frank Field argued on grounds of fairness that those who had paid sufficient rent to cover the build costs of their home should be granted ownership of it. Moreover, some Local Authority landlords represented bureaucratic paternalism at its worst: inefficient, with poor service and harshly prescriptive tenancy conditions. These conditions were seized upon by the Conservatives, who sold the right to buy as freedom from landlordism and the freedom to choose the colour of one's front door – the symbolism of a far wider freedom to seize control of both everyday domestic life and future aspirations for home and family.

Of course, landlordism was equally objectionable to many on the left. And there was also considerable scope for the left to have taken the right to buy and made it its own – a central vehicle for both greater asset equality, and the social equality and freedom that could flow from this. Indeed, the politics of the right to buy revolved around just such deep issues of principle: contested views of 'freedom' and 'equality', as well as the proper constitution and role of the state.

As we shall shortly see, these issues of ideology and contested principle played a vital role in shaping the attitudes and perceptions that drove the continuing residualisation of the tenure.

But there were also far more prosaic and visible processes at work. The legislation for the right to buy was a key turning point in the residualisation of social housing for two key reasons. Firstly, it led to mass exit from public tenure of great numbers of those able to exercise the right to purchase their home. Immediately, this sent out a powerful signal about the nature of public housing: it was the tenure of the poor and dependent. Over time, it also led to exit not just from the tenure, but often from the neighbourhoods that were once 'respectable' council estates. The very steep discounts allowed individuals to later sell their ex-council homes for great profits, which were then used to gain as much physical and social distance as possible from council estates and any reminders of council tenancy.

Moreover, this outflow and decline in the number of households in the social sector did not, as one might reasonably expect, ease the pressure on supply. The legislation for the right to buy was not just about a particular vision of individual freedom and opportunity; it was also a central mechanism in 'rolling back the state'. Thus, the 1980 Act set punitive terms on Local Authorities and greatly restricted their ability to use receipts from sales to reinvest in replenishing lost council stock; typically, and naturally enough, the best stock – the kind of Bevan-era housing that typical families might now aspire to own. Instead of using sales to build more quality of housing, receipts were to be used to pay down debt and thus shrink the size of the state.

So while the 1977 Act created greater demand for public housing (without a commensurate increase in supply), the 1980 Act, reduced demand but also reduced the supply of public housing, leading to a shrunken stock that, more than ever, was reserved only for the very needy.

Yet the impact of the right to buy was not simply a structural one: its pernicious effects ran deeper than the greatly diminished supply of social housing and the subsequent concentration of poverty. In the terms of a Thatcherite property owning democracy there was also a clear condemnation of the needy themselves.

This is of course a theme that stretches back throughout the history we have traced. But the Thatcherite turn took the age old schema of the deserving and undeserving poor and tied it to both 'freedom' and 'citizenship'. On the one hand, the right to buy was presented as an opportunity for the individual to 'free' themselves from the paternalism and control of the state; it was a vision of moral and economic independence. On the other hand, however, this independence was not just a right and an opportunity; it was also a duty not to be a burden on the state and other taxpayers. The failure to grasp it was a moral failing – an inability or refusal to take up the responsibilities of the full citizen. This sentiment is expressed most clearly in Thatcher's own astonishing words: council houses were "breeding grounds of socialism, dependency, vandalism and crime"; whereas home ownership taught "all the virtues of good citizenship".[34]

The fullest proof of this freedom and responsibility was, clearly, the ability and willingness to leave the tenure of social housing and strike out as independent property owning citizen. Those that did not were both less free themselves and a burden on the freedom of others. Untangling the conceptual subtleties and confusions of this schema is a task in itself, but for our purposes the salient point is that the Thatcherite vision of freedom sent out a resounding message about the desirability and status of social housing; it was the tenure of second class citizens. Exit, and social distance, was the mark of respectability and acceptance in society.

The story told in this chapter may seem unremittingly negative. It has been a history of poor planning and poor supply, an allocations system that compounds the problems of poverty and public housing, and a system of beliefs and prejudices that condemns a large portion of our fellow citizens to the category of second class citizens. Yet, as we saw in the opening chapter, there is no *necessary* connection between public housing and poverty: experience of growing up in council housing for those born in 1946 (the very same year that Bevan's vision of mix was in the process of being brought to fruition) had no effect on future life chances. In the following chapter we shall examine the problems that need to be overcome if we are to return to Bevan's vision and make it a reality.

3 | Residualisation and poverty

S o, the story of public housing in England since 1945 is a mixed one: significant moments of expansion and improvement punctuating a trajectory of decline and residualisation. But why should this residualisation have resulted in the detrimental link between public housing and life chances, examined in Chapter 1? Certainly, residualisation seems an undesirable phenomenon in itself; but why should it work as a driver of poverty and disadvantage, and what are the causal mechanisms underpinning this?

This relates to a more general question about poverty and welfare: why is it that highly targeted welfare systems perform so poorly in terms of poverty prevention? 'Liberal' welfare systems, such as that of the US, and to some extent Australia, Ireland and the UK, which are characterised, among other things, by a high degree of targeting and means testing, tend to perform significantly worse than more universalist and even insurance-based welfare systems in terms of poverty and inequality.[35]

Recent academic research has rightly been cautious about inferring causal processes from some of the compelling correlations observed between housing tenure, poverty and disadvantage. But, as international comparative studies show, across all welfare sectors – from housing to income support to healthcare – highly residualised welfare provision is not only typically ineffective in tackling poverty, it often seems to entrench and trap recipients in poverty, with the welfare institutions themselves becoming a 'structural cause' of poverty and disadvantage.

Understanding why these differences in performance exist between different welfare systems, that is, how particular design principles relate to policy effectiveness, should be a key priority for welfare state reform. But beyond looking at obvious differences in the *generosity* of these welfare states, comparative welfare state studies have not been particularly forthcoming about the causal mechanisms underlying these differences in performance.

In this chapter we seek to investigate the general causal mechanisms underpinning this link between welfare system design and welfare outcomes in the case of residualisation. The section below outlines a general cross-sectoral framework for looking at the behaviours and institutional properties that underpin these causal mechanisms. This is then followed by an exploration of these processes at work within the sphere of public housing.

The effects of residualisation

The fact that countries with highly targeted systems of welfare perform relatively poorly in terms of poverty at first seems something of a paradox. All things being equal, a high concentration of generous benefits on the poorest is redistributionally efficient – and so should be maximally effective from the perspective of poverty prevention.

The key to understanding why a high degree of targeting is often ineffective lies in the insight that different choices of distributive strategy and institutional design not only have distributional effects; they have relational effects too. For example, different principles of allocation (needs-based, contribution-based, etc.) will imply different types of relationships between people (solidaristic, competitive, etc.), some of which may be more desirable in particular contexts than others.[36] And different shapes of service coverage or different criteria of service eligibility will structure the population into corresponding groups (recipients – non-recipients or eligible – non-eligible), which, again, may or may not be desirable. And in many situations, these relational effects can have consequences which work against the distributional benefits of targeting.

Herein lies the classic dilemma about the appropriate balance of universalism and selectivism for effective anti-poverty policy. And the lesson of welfare history is that it is necessary to balance the way in which system coverage, allocation levels and allocation principles are geared to achieving redistributive efficiency, on the one hand, against their propensity to segment the population into different groups, on the other.

The relational effects of residualisation

As well as its impact on distribution, the targeting of resources structures the relationships between individuals within society. In particular, it divides people into distinct groups on the basis of an institutional categorisation – usually as recipients or non-recipients.

The process of residualisation – such as a narrowing in the base of public housing tenants, which becomes increasingly concentrated amongst the poorest – serves to make these institutional divisions particularly acute. Broadly speaking, there are two types of effect that occur as a result: a *labelling effect* and a *separation effect* , both of which can have potentially detrimental consequences for policy effectiveness over the short and the long term.

Labelling effects – immediate

Labelling effects influence policy effectiveness by affecting *social identity*. When institutions provide differential treatment for different groups – whether on the basis of housing tenure, labour market categorisation, benefit receipt, type of school, or whatever – this, if salient, can result in the social categorisation of people into 'ingroups' and 'outgroups'. This is particularly the case when the targeting applies to a small minority of the population. For welfare targeted at the poorest, it creates an 'othering' of the poor.

Robust academic research on the psychology of group dynamics backs this point up. Experimental psychology has shown that negative categorisations tends to lead to a strong identity formation in the group that has not been stigmatised; and that the perceived identity of the ingroup relies heavily on an shared emphasis on the positive characteristics that mark it off as superior to the stigmatised outgroup.[37] This is not just a matter of concern for those that care about the internal lives and sense of worth of these so called 'out-groups'; it has important practical consequences too. One of the forms that this can take is discrimination in job applications, and there is also evidence of postcode discrimination when job applications are being assessed.[38] But we only have to consider the media language and coverage of 'chavs' to see beyond these specific examples and see just how culturally pervasive the sense of discrimination is.

Labelling effects – long term

Over the longer term, the social categorisation of people into different groups driven by selectivism in policy can have detrimental effects on solidarity and public willingness to redistribute to other groups. At its most extreme, group membership can generate 'moral exclusion' for outgroups – where people simply do not see the disadvantaged as part of their 'community of responsibility'.[39] More generally, however, the social distance created by institutional cleavages affects individuals' evaluations of distributive (and procedural) fairness in social dilemmas, including their willingness to redistribute.[40] Some of these results have recently been taken up in political science to explain support for or opposition to welfare policy, such as in explicating the link between identity and perceptions of deservingness.[41]

In Table 1, Larsen (2007) demonstrates a strong correlation between the degree of selectivism in a country's welfare regime and public support for welfare for the poorest, with significantly lower levels of support for welfare in more selective regimes.

	Denmark	Finland	Norway	Sweden
Housing allowance coverage* (share of population; %)	5.7	7.5	1.1	8.0
Measure of stigma towards those claiming housing allowances** (% saying those claiming such benefits are looked down upon. Share of population; %)	10	17	23	12
Social assistance coverage (share of population; %)	5.8	9.0	4.5	5.5
Measure of stigma towards those claiming social assistance (% saying those claiming such benefits are looked down upon)	73	49	70	68

Table 1 Correlation between selectivism and public support. Larsen

* Coverage here refers to the percentage of the population covered by the benefit.
** The measure of stigma here is based on the percentage of the population answering that the benefit draws stigma 'very often' or 'often', 'quite rarely' or 'rarely'.

Note: The results in the table reflect the hypothesis that selectivity in welfare distribution leads to stigmatisation i.e. the more selective and targeted a measure it is, the greater degree of stigma. The results are based on a survey in which respondents were questioned on their attitudes to recipients of certain measures, particularly the extent to which people 'looked down' on these individuals. As we see above, there is indeed a connection. Norway provides targeted housing assistance to far fewer people than in the other countries, and there is a correspondingly greater proportion of the population that 'looks down' on the recipients. A similar relationship is clear for those in receipt of social assistance.

Separation effects – immediate

Separation effects influence policy effectiveness by affecting *individual capability* or *autonomy*. In addition to its effects on social identity, the institutional division of people into groups often imposes different sets of circumstances on them. In particular, people that are the recipients of a targeted policy will, along with the extra resources or services they get, inherit a set of circumstances or conditions that apply precisely in virtue of receiving those resources, and which therefore separate them from non-recipients.

If designed poorly, these conditions can then impose *barriers* on a recipient's ability to move out of the state that qualifies them to be in receipt of targeted support. An obvious example of this is benefit withdrawal, whereby moving up the income scale subjects the recipient to high marginal effective tax rates, potentially acting as a disincentive to earning more money and creating a 'poverty trap'.

Separation effects – long term

As well as creating immediate barriers to exit from poverty, over the longer term separation effects can diminish an individual's capability to exit from poverty by normalising separation and generating a *culture of detachment*. Here, the cumulative effects of separation become entrenched in a way that undermines an individual's autonomy and limits their options. To cite a recently discussed example, if the conditions of incapacity benefit receipt require demonstration of inability to work and absolute separation from the labour market, this can, over time, diminish an individual's ability to re-enter the labour market, through loss of skills, confidence, motivation, and so on. Or, if an individual has been used to planning finances around the receipt of a benefit, the prospect of having it withdrawn, and the instability that could result, might be a strong disincentive to take up opportunities.[42] Instead, it is crucial that the receipt of welfare promotes attachment to the conditions, services, information, etc., that increase an individual's capability to exit from poverty.

(A crucial caveat is in order here, however. The phenomenon I have been describing is to be sharply distinguished from common ascriptions of 'dependency', where the receipt of benefits or services is somehow itself held to be morally dubious – and the end goal is seen as independence from benefits or services. In our vision, receipt of collective financial support or services is not necessarily a condition to exit from (which is, after all, why we have universal benefits and services); rather the aim is to exit from poverty.) The issues discussed above are summarised in Table 2.

The factors identified above all suggest why, across different welfare sectors, a highly selective and residualised model of welfare provision can ultimately be ineffective, despite its redistributive efficiency.

Type of effect	labelling effects	separation effects
Mediating factor	*imposed social categorisation*	*reduced capability/ autonomy/incentives*
Immediate consequences	stigmatisation and corresponding social behaviours	conditions that create barriers to exit from poverty
Long-term consequences	reduction in public willingness to redistribute to the disadvantaged group	conditions that normalise detachment from the circumstances required to exit from poverty

Table 2 Effects that limit the effectiveness of selectivism in welfare policy

Behaviours resulting from stigma affect both the recipients of welfare themselves and broader public support for welfare institutions and distribution. One of the clearest examples of the first set of behaviours is the phenomenon of low take-up: the stigma attached to some benefits can prevent those that most need them from actually claiming the benefit. Another example is the way in which the *withdrawal* of highly targeted benefits impacts upon individual behaviour: steep withdrawal rates act as a disincentive to work as a route out of poverty. And public perceptions (and incomplete understanding) of this 'refusal' to work alter the behaviour and attitudes of the mass of citizens that must support the welfare state if it is not be in perpetual crisis of legitimacy.

Exploring the consequences of these effects in public housing

What is the evidence for these processes of labelling and separation in the sphere of public housing, and what impact do they have on poverty and disadvantage?

Separation effects

Perhaps the most easily recognisable problem facing public housing is *spatial separation* . This includes, but goes beyond, the fact that much public housing is spatially concentrated in particular areas and in large estates. Much of it is also served by poor infrastructure and is detached from labour markets. In part this is the result of macro-economic changes leading to the decline of local industries. Yet equally often such estates have been built without a pre-existing labour market, and without adequate transport infrastructure to make jobs accessible.

All this is forgivable, perhaps, when we recall that many of the isolated estates were built in the interwar years, with planning lessons yet to be learnt the hard way. But there is no excuse for the same mistake to be made today. And it is: much of the Thames Gateway Growth Area is being built with poor transport infrastructure and with an approach to planning that often seems to rob Peter in order to pay Paul. In Barking Riverside, for example, the development was provided with a new bus route, but it was not really new at all, merely diverted away from the nearest council estate.[43] This is a stark illustration of a more general phenomenon that is already making the Thames Gateway notorious amongst public housing providers: even where the quality of the housing is itself good, the overall planning (and viability) of estates is typically based on the assumption that the ideal resident will not just be home-owning, but car owning too. Physical separation and isolation is therefore a very real barrier to work. One may be filtered into such an isolated neighbourhood, but exit from poverty is then made all the harder by the physical isolation itself.

Spatial separation also brings with it a loss of access to many public and consumer services. The following example is typical of the experience of many who have lived on or visited large council estates. When the Greater London Council completed the Elthorne Estate in London's Islington in 1978, the number of shops left to service the local population had fallen from nearly a hundred to just three.[44] A slum clearance program had in effect raised the cost of eating: it left in place a commercial monopoly in which there was no competition (or choice) that could drive down consumer prices. Those estates we see with one forlorn convenience store aren't an accident of fate, they are a consequence of poor planning design, design that very often compounds poverty.

Market forces don't help either. In 2004 a National Consumer Council report found that low income households 'pay more or get less across a range of essential services'.[45] Charging cash machines and expensive local shops immediately jump out as examples, but there is a whole range of services for which households in deprived communities pay more: for food, water, energy, communication, banking and loans. In part this is because cash is not king – paying bills via a cash meter, for example, costs more than by direct debit. But, more generally, both the NCC report and a more recent (2007) American study of poverty in

Kentucky come to the same broad conclusion; that the logic of the 'free-market' systematically discriminates against poor areas.[46]

To put it simply, businesses follow the money and don't compete for the custom of the poor. The net result is that low income households not only have less money, but are also more stretched in what they can actually do with it. And all of this is, of course, compounded by the lack of transport infrastructure that we have just described. Competition and choice mean nothing without physical access.

One might think that, in contrast to commercial services, concentrations of poverty attract public services. This is indeed true, and there has been a great deal of improvement in recent years under the Labour government via area-based initiatives such as the New Deal for Communities and the Neighbourhood Renewal Fund, with evidence that this has also improved the quality of life in some areas.[47]

So we should not succumb to a council of despair. Nevertheless, it remains the case that public services in deprived areas are often poor too, overwhelmed by the sheer weight of demand, with high attrition rates amongst staff worn down by the demands of the job. Of the utmost importance is the chronic lack of adequate advisory services that deal with individual problems holistically and comprehensively. These problems range across the spectrum of multiple disadvantage and cover everything from housing needs and rights, financial advice and assistance, health needs and employment and education opportunities.

In the context of consumer services, there is an urgent need to connect households to good financial advisory services, which all too often can't match the vigour and 'advice' of loan sharks. Debt very often costs more for low-income households (who often do not fulfil the lending criteria of mainstream providers), and is one of the key triggers that lead households to slip into income poverty (and then keep them there).[48,49] Typically, debt arises to meet everyday living costs when benefits are not sufficient, and very often it is a financial shock beyond the individual's control that leads to the debt.[50] Once again, this is both a form and symptom of social exclusion, in the sense that these households are denied the goods and security that we all take for granted; and, crucially, a potential cause and key risk factor when sudden uninsured losses create a financial crisis that can trigger a spiral into debt and income poverty. It took the floods of 2007 for this aspect of household poverty to become widely recognised, yet we still fail to provide any form of specific state assistance in understanding or obtaining basic household insurance.

These barriers of separation also exist in other aspects of housing welfare, such as Housing Benefit, where the steep withdrawal of the benefit (with 65p of every extra pound from work withdrawn) can disincentivise work participation and progression, and the complexity of its administration can result in uncertainty, which can in turn act as a barrier to work.[51, 52] (See 'Housing Benefit' section on page 70).

Labelling effects

Distinct from these separation effects are a set of labelling effects akin to those described at the outset of this chapter (though the physical segregation of social tenants in large estates only increases the visibility of households' 'welfare clientele' status, making such labelling effects even more acute),

Here, there is ample evidence that part of the disadvantage created by place and tenure is the direct result of stigma and discrimination. We see this very clearly in the phenomenon of postcode discrimination in the jobs market, for example.

Thus, a recent Department of Work and Pensions report found that those living in the concentrated public housing of Sheffield's Manor Estate did indeed experience postcode discrimination in the labour market. Perceptions of fecklessness excluded these individuals at the earliest stages of the applications process, and the failure is attributed to the individual rather than the employer – thereby entrenching the perception that it is individual fecklessness that is to blame.[53] The same postcode discrimination is present in the provision of consumer services too. Both credit and insurance can (and often are) denied solely on the basis of postcode, with a premium that is inflated even when we consider the higher crime rates of deprived areas.[54, 55]

Further categorisation and labelling takes place within the population of social tenants. As we saw in the previous chapter, there is a long history of Local Authorities separating tenants into the two categories of 'respectable' and 'problem' tenants. In part this is driven by an understandable desire to isolate some anti-social households from those seeking peace. Nevertheless, it further concentrates the most disadvantaged and chaotic households in small areas, and thus overburdens services and helps create the norms and expectations that actually make anti-social behaviour far harder to deal with.

Moreover, we must also recognise that the scarcity of public housing has led to a rationing system that has the perverse result of encouraging 'self-labelling'. Our needs-based allocation system is based on a points system that incentivises individuals to 'present' as needy, and to thereby fulfil some of the stereotypes of a dependent underclass. In this way, a highly residualised system can actually encourage and maintain the disadvantage it is supposed to combat.

What about the consequences of these labelling effects for public attitudes over the longer term? Polling for the Fabian Society and L&Q Housing reveals broader identity effects in attitudes to public housing tenants. A significant minority (around a third) of the population felt that those living on large council estates aren't like them (including 38 per cent of people who don't have a large council estate in their area). Those who feel this way rank such tenants low in terms of deservingness (see the first two questions in the table below), with effects on both their attitudes towards wanting to mix with social tenants and their willingness to support redistribution nationally (see the last two questions).

Culture and separation

We have seen that there are a number of ways in which public housing tenants undergo labelling and separation. The labelling contributes to –

and reinforces – the separation, and the separation in turn reinforces the assumptions of the labelling in a negative feedback loop; thereby undermining support poverty prevention measures, and ultimately becoming part of the structural causes of poverty over the long-term.

	Those who feel they have 'a lot' / 'a little' in common with those living on council estates	Those who feel they have 'not very much'/ 'nothing' in common with those living on council estates
People living on council estates are working hard to get on in life..		
Agree	50	24
Disagree	13	30
People living on council estates make responsible decisions about spending and saving money.		
Agree	32	13
Disagree	21	40
Do you think mixed communities are a good idea?[56]		
Good idea	59	36
Bad idea	37	60
The Government should spend more on welfare benefits for the poor, even if it leads to higher taxes...		
Agree	43	30
Disagree	35	47

But there is something else going on here too. It is not just poor infra-structure and services and lack of access to jobs that accounts for the strong correlation between public housing and disadvantage. There is something about the 'culture' of deprived areas that itself entrenches disadvantage and acts as a barrier to an exit from poverty. Over time, this separation and its consequences can become the norm within a community, especially in communities that have very high concentra-tions of chronic, and intergenerational, worklessness. The social norm can then become the individual expectation, curbing aspiration and suppressing motivation.

Indeed, whilst numerous studies have found, time and again, that there has been no absence of 'social capital' in these communities. On the contrary, many have thick, supportive social networks; the 'bonding capital' that helps to maintain the identity of an area and a thick sense of solidarity.[57] But they can also tend to be inward looking and parochial, isolated from other neighbourhoods; ripe terrain for a social dynamic to develop in which there is no expectation either of work or of exit.[58] And in the absence of 'bridging social capital' linking these communities to wider social networks and information, it has often proved very difficult to break these pernicious patterns of social norms of worklessness.

Anecdotal evidence from EC1, the New Deal for Communities project in Islington, tells the same, powerful story about housing separation and segregation: right on the doorstep of Canary Wharf, many of the young public housing tenants have never knowingly left the postcode, such is the limitation of their social horizons.[59] It is a story that one hears, time and again, in nearly all of the most deprived communities: not at all an absence of community spirit, but an absence of connection with the wider community. On the Stanhope estate near Ashford in Kent, a purpose built Local Authority estate, set on the edge of Ashford like a small town, the local Sure Start is underused and for one simple reason – it is on the wrong side of the ring-road that marks the limits of a very local territory.

To conclude, we have explored the general ways in which the residualisation of welfare creates and entrenches poverty and shown the operation of these mechanisms in the context of public housing. These include both the consequences of policies which label public housing tenants as a special group and the consequences of policies which separate tenants from the rest of the population (whether in spatial terms or resource terms), imposing barriers to exit from poverty and potentially generating a culture of detachment.

This analysis suggests that the appropriate policy responses to the residualisation of public housing will need to combat these labelling and separation effects which too often serve to segregate social tenants from the rest of the population.

4 | Policy solutions

In the previous chapter we saw how the Anglo-Saxon model of highly targeted welfare provision has a strong tendency to add to the causal processes driving poverty. This perverse consequence is a result of the dual 'labelling' and 'separation effects' I described, with institutions categorising and marking out 'the poor' in a way that encourages us to think of the poor as somehow 'other', stigmatised as feckless and undeserving, and separated from mainstream society. This, in turn, creates a crisis of welfare legitimacy: where there is a perception that welfare claimants are undeserving, it becomes harder to move away from the excessive targeting that actually entrenches these public perceptions of poverty.

Thus, the central message of the last chapter was that welfare for the poor leads to poor welfare. The policy strategies recommended in this chapter are explicitly designed to maintain a degree of targeting where this is indeed the fairest and most efficient means of welfare delivery, but to do so in a framework that is not caught in the trap of these labelling and separation effects.

Policy solutions to welfare residualisation: strategic approaches

Whilst it is neither possible nor desirable to provide public housing as a universal service for all, it is of the utmost importance that whatever degree of targeting that we necessarily pursue does not lead to the negative effects we have described thus far. Public housing must not be part of a systemic process in which selection creates perceptions of 'in' and 'out' groups, in which social tenants are considered to be somehow 'other' and not socially equal to their fellow citizens.

In the previous chapter, we looked at two main ways in which the current provision of public housing can 'segregate' social tenants from the rest of society. The first was a spatial phenomenon, whereby tenants can be geographically isolated and separated from other households, jobs, services, and so on – whether specifically on large council estates or in poorer areas more generally. The second was a polarisation in tenure itself, especially between (though not limited to) social tenants and owner occupiers, a division which underpins both differences in social status and inequalities in household wealth.

In spatial terms, universality and integration implies we must pursue a policy of housing mix. This will of course mean insisting on new developments being mixed communities. But 'mix' here also means far more than a policy of new mixed developments. Indeed, if we focus too narrowly on mixed developments we risk these becoming, at best, seen as exceptional pockets of best practice in a still deeply residualised sector and, at worst, strange walled cities cut off from the rest of society.

Taken on their own, 'mixed communities', though vitally important, are not sufficient to address the depth of the problems we are facing. What is needed is a wider, and deeper, sense of mix. Thus, the first principle underlying the argument in this chapter is that we must insist *on mix in its deepest sense* . This will also involve pursuing mix for existing estates, which can be mixed through active management policies. And, over time, we must insist on the full social and physical integration of public housing within the stock of private housing in England. In practice, this means having the funds and political will to buy and build public housing in Chelsea as well as in Brixton.

The point of this integration is to reconnect the social housing tenure to our mainstream housing stock, and to put an end to spatial isolation and segregation. But other forms of connection are vital too: whilst the end of spatial segregation is itself a matter of social justice, the impact on poverty will be limited if disadvantaged households are not supported through active interventions that address long-term worklessness and exclusion from labour markets.

Of course, if there are no labour markets to connect to, or if they are hard to access by transport, advice and support will be relatively futile. We all know what is needed: wise and imaginative planning, and communities that are properly connected to both public and private services, providing tenants with better access to jobs, transport and affordable public services. But we also know that while these principles are well established, too often they are neglected in practice. So where mixed communities and other planning solutions prove impossible, interventions will be necessary to reconnect tenants with information, opportunities and services as routes out of poverty.

Thus, a second key principle of housing policy must be that *housing is not just about a decent home, it must also be used as a vehicle of broader service delivery*. Applications of this principle include, for example, holistic housing management that offers employment services as well as the more typical housing services, with the aim of reconnecting tenants to labour markets. Government should also work with industry providers to ensure better availability of services in low-income neighbourhoods (such as the recent Treasury initiative to ensure wider access to free cash machines).

Finally, a third principle advocated here is that *tenure should not be a marker of social status*. In the short-term, this requires that tenure distinctions should be made less visible and relevant. All new public housing, both in mixed communities and in the broader housing supply, should not only be integrated with other tenures, it should also be indistinguishable from other tenures. This, of course, does not mean that we must all live in mansions. But what a policy of 'tenure blindness' does mean is that a social tenure flat or house must be indistinguishable from a private property that is comparable in size, and which conforms to high standards of design and build quality. The best way to achieve this is through a general policy of 'pepper potting' – the practice of making private and social residents direct next door neighbours – wherever practically possible, rather than the clustering of public housing units. Indeed, the formation of tenure-blind mixed communities has been shown to reduce stigma, with individuals in different tenures over-whelmingly regarding one another as 'ordinary people' – thereby removing an important factor (perceived social distance) that is known to create stigma and reduce support for welfare policy.[60] Moreover, studies have found that mixed tenure communities are both commer-cially viable from a developers' perspective and popular with private purchasers, with house prices in these developments matching or outperforming the local market.

The principle that tenure should not mark social status has more radical implications for the long-term. With the exception of a very small amount of shared equity housing (in which the occupant shares ownership with the landlord), we have become stuck in a binary oppo-sition between 'ownership' and 'non-ownership'. As we have seen, this has taken on very powerful political and normative connotations, which strengthen social separation between tenures and reinforce the stigma of the social rented sector. Ultimately, the ideal of tenure blindness should therefore extend beyond planning and the spatial location of tenure, and lead to the reclassification of all property tenures.

But the common theme running throughout the three principles I have elucidated here is the foundational principle of reconnection and integration, the opposite of the labelling and separation effects I have described throughout this pamphlet.

Let us now turn to the first of these three principles; that public housing must be fully integrated with other tenures. The clearest way to test these principles is through an examination of the existing evidence on planned mixed communities. However, nearly all of the lessons apply directly to the broader aim of mix across the housing stock, outside of self-contained developments.

Section 1 – Achieving *real* mixed communities

What we know about mix

Over the last five years, the idea of 'mixed communities' has received a lot of attention in policy discussions. It is a policy idea that has the potential to sharply divide opinion. At one extreme there can be an almost utopian faith in the power of mix. The idealist advocate of mix may hope, with a certain naivety, for rich social interaction across class and tenure; with a thick sense of community that provides the role models that lead the poor out of their poverty. At the other extreme, there are those that argue that 'social capital' and 'mixed communities' are all hot air, a distraction from dealing with the key cause of poverty: economic inequality and income poverty.[61] In this view, a policy of mix merely treats the symptoms rather than the causes of poverty.

In fact, a brief review of the evidence justifies neither of these caricatures. And once we have a clearer idea of what we can expect mix to achieve we can begin to advocate a far clearer policy framework.

Thus far, the evidence we have on mix has yielded the seemingly prosaic but in fact very important conclusion that residents of established mixed communities regard one another as 'ordinary people'.[62] There was no stigma attached to tenancy. Indeed, a separate interview-based study of the attitudes of homeowners on a mixed estate found that 89 per cent were satisfied with their neighbourhood, and when prompted to respond directly to the question of *income* mix (a far better proxy of social mix than tenure alone), 53 per cent of owners felt it made no difference to their satisfaction, and 24 per cent had a positive view of mix.[63] What *did* count in terms of satisfaction were quality homes, good services and a feeling that the neighbourhood was pleasant and safe.

We also know that these positive reactions are not just internal: good planned mix – both new developments and active interventions in older neighbourhoods – has generated positive perceptions of neighbourhoods from those living outside, and from those seeking to move in. This is often reflected in the property values of mixed areas. Open market price increases in some developments (for example, New Earswick) have outperformed the regional average, and across seven case studies there was no significant negative association in which mix drives down property prices.[64,65] Again, in all cases, far more significant than mix in terms of the attractiveness of the neighbourhood was the quality of the homes and the surrounding infrastructure and services. Moreover, private developers, by and large, acknowledge this, and believe that it is the quality of the build and the neighbourhood space that is of paramount importance for marketability.[66]

What is of crucial importance here is the loss of stigma: these are neighbourhoods of choice, not of last resort. And there is ample evidence that both internal and external perceptions of such neighbourhoods and the self-image of public housing tenants can be significantly improved.[67] As we have seen, this is not merely about making tenants feel better: if mixed communities are popular and viable, we can begin to really tackle some of the deep spatial and social segregation that are part of the causal processes of poverty.

So mix matters in very practical terms – it breaks up the physical concentrations of poverty that are not only a symptomatic reflection of poverty, but also act as a barrier to exit from poverty. And it matters in a deeper sense too. We saw in Chapter 3 that those who feel that council estate tenants aren't like them rank such tenants low in terms of deservingness, with a corresponding decrease in their support for related welfare measures. And further analysis of the data revealed another crucial point: the fewer social tenants an individual knew, and the further they lived from a council estate, the less they identified with council tenants (and so the less inclined theuy were to support measures to help them).

Thus, in the context of the history of stigma and residualisation, we should not underestimate the achievements of mix thus far: that we are managing to build good public housing in communities where tenants are regarded as 'ordinary' people. Breaking down the stigma of tenure not only has a positive impact on existing tenants, it can also help to

51

negate the more abstract but deeply entrenched perception that public housing is a valueless public good: at best the last resort of the desperate, at worst a drain on the public purse.

Ordinariness is an in fact an extraordinary achievement.

There is, however, a crucial caveat that we must enter here. For the most ardent advocates of mix, 'ordinariness' is something of a disappointment. Early advocates of mix hoped that there would be strong peer effects', in which the more affluent would act as positive role models, especially as active participants in the labour market. They also hoped for a far deeper sense of human interaction; mix was to grow the stock of social capital and lead to a flourishing of local civic activity and duty.

Unfortunately, the evidence we have from the UK is not yet sufficient to confirm this. Most tangibly, studies of mix in the UK have not found any positive impact on work-rates.[68] Nor have they found much evidence of genuine interaction across tenures. Mix, then, has indeed been quite quiet and prosaic – a process of normalisation rather than a utopian dream.

But this is not to say that the hypothesised connection between mix and lower rates of worklessness is false. Part of the problem is that we are very bad at tracking the relevant data in the UK.[69] The great body of work that we have on mix tends to be based on case studies and qualitative evidence rather than hard statistical correlations. Indeed, when we turn to Sweden, a country that does scrupulously collect the data, there is good evidence of the benefits of mix on employment rates.

Social researchers in Sweden have access to datasets that cover the entire population. This allows researchers to control for a wide range of individual variables in order to ensure that any imputed causal relationship between area and unemployment is not better explained by other factors. This is particularly important when we consider the possibility that poverty and worklessness is concentrated in certain areas not because the area itself is part of the causal story of poverty, but because the poor and workless are filtered into these areas. Yet this is proven *not* to be the case in an important Swedish study which looked at more than 5.5 million individuals.

Studying all individuals of working age (16 to 65) from 1991 to 1999, Sako Musterd and Roger Andersson found robust evidence that the neighbourhood in which individuals live clearly did have an impact on their employment prospects.[70] In other words, it is not just that those living in such areas may be disconnected form labour markets in spatial terms (though this is indeed the case); there is also something about living amongst other unemployed households that has an impact on worklessness, even when it may seem that there are good opportunities in local labour markets.[71] Very clearly, social capital (the norms and expectations of a very local culture) can have a profound impact. In this case the impact of that social capital is negative rather than positive. Musterd and Andersson thus draw two specific conclusions that weigh heavily in favour of the hypothesis that mix must be part of the corrective to concentrated poverty and poor individual life-chances.

Firstly, even controlling for alternate factors and explanations, "the risk that a person unemployed in 1991 would still be unemployed in 1995 and 1999 is only 16% if that person lives in an environment with only 0–2% unemployed people, whereas that percentage would double to 32% if he or she lives in an environment with 14–16% unemployed."[72]

Secondly, the same phenomenon is also evident in the parallel conclusion that "the probability that a person unemployed in 1991 would succeed in becoming employed in 1995 and 1999 is 56% if that person lives in an environment with only 0–2% unemployed people; if he or she lives in an environment with 14–16% unemployment, the probability does not exceed 35%!"[73]

In a follow-up study, the authors pursue this further and test the strength of the neighbourhood effect when the means of measurement is varied. What they found was that income-structure yielded the strongest neighbourhood effect, ahead of (for example) education levels.[74] Income structure was particularly important in dense urban contexts, where the concentrations of low income households is most marked. Hence, the study finds that individual incomes are affected by "the socio-economic composition of the neighbourhoods".[75] Mix, the study concludes, really *does* matter.

Of course, we cannot simply translate the evidence from Sweden to the British context. There will be important variables – different histories of stigma (or pride) associated with public housing, different welfare institutions, different labour markets, and so on. We should also not forget that housing and income mix alone cannot be a silver bullet for the problems of entrenched poverty. Clearly, there are some obvious limits to what we can reasonably expect of a policy framework of housing mix. It is therefore vital that mix is part of a wider framework of policy solutions that tackle poverty head-on, in the here and now.

But mixed income communities must be the central structure within that framework. This conclusion is not based upon a utopian hankering after a fluffy feeling of cross-class solidarity and community: it is based on the emerging, hard evidence on the impact of social segregation. That hard evidence on worklessness is not yet available in the UK; but given the relatively greater generosity and activism of the Swedish welfare state compared to ours, there is every reason to believe that the same neighbourhood affect will be found here – once we start collecting the relevant data in a systematic way.

Planning for mix

Supply
There are two distinct, but intimately related, issues here. The first is that much of the residualisation of public housing has been driven by a chronic and increasingly acute lack of supply. At present, there are approximately 1.7 million households on the waiting list for public housing. With a large enough increase in supply, some of the processes of residualisation would automatically be reversed, for the simple reason that more people, and a greater social range, would be brought into the tenure.

In the Housing Green Paper of July 2007, the Labour Government announced a key target for general housing supply: 3 million new homes were to be built by 2020, with 240, 000 new homes being built a year by 2016. They also recognised that approximately 40,000 new social homes would be needed per year (net) in order to meet housing need.[76]

Yet in November of last year, build completions were down to the lowest level in three decades, at below half the rate of new builds in 2006. Clearly, it would be absurd to accuse the Government of a lack of will here, since we are in the midst of perhaps the most spectacular housing crash for generations.

Nevertheless, there has been a fundamental strategic flaw in the provision of public housing over the last decade: it has relied too extensively on partnerships with private developers, in which Local Authorities use so-called 'Section 106' planning agreements to encourage developers to include a proportion of social (and affordable) housing in their private developments. The logic was simple: no planning permission without the 106 agreement. But the logic was also fatal in a falling market: if the developers could not sell the private units they could not cross-subsidise the social homes. Social provision thus collapsed with the private market.

We might expect the Housing Associations to pick up the slack here. Unfortunately, the Government's strategy here has also been flawed. Housing Associations have increasingly been encouraged to act as private developers. With as little as 30 per cent of their development costs coming from public housing grants, the rest has had to be raised from money markets as corporate debt, and through commercial sales on the open market, using the profit to finance their public housing provision. Like the 106 strategy, it has now failed.

Thus, over the last ten years the supply of public housing has been driven by a strategy that is only viable in a rising market. Both private developers and Housing Associations have used market profit to cross-subsidise public housing. The collapse of the market has now left us with a complete collapse of public housing supply, adding to the severe supply constraints of the last thirty years. We need a new policy framework that both offers alternative sources of supply, and which makes better use of private-public developer collaboration when the housing market recovers, thereby greatly increasing supply in the medium term.

The first alternative source of supply should come from allowing Local Authorities to bid directly for Housing Grant, to raise money through bonds, and to act as a developer and private landlord in their own right. This would be both an alternative source of supply and offer a local means of managing mix and tying in housing services to other services, especially employment and training. There have been very welcome moves in this direction lately, and it has recently been announced that councils will indeed be able to bid for Housing Grant money.[77] The challenge now is to ensure that the (as yet unspecified) conditions under which they can do so are not too tightly circumscribed.

A second source of alternative supply involves the creation of a number of national house-builders. In the current climate, with many private builders in distress, there will be considerable private sector appetite for it. We should establish a small number of joint venture public-private home builders, each with a 50 per cent stake and an equal share of the profits. The national share would be reinvested directly in public housing (in accordance with the principles of mix), and the private partner will be able to deliver reasonable profits to shareholders, whilst also being obliged to maintain prudent levels of investment in the operating capacity and capital structure of the business. Such companies would be commercial concerns with the public shareholding expected to turn as much profit as the private component; and they will be profitable so long as it pursues the modern Housing Association strategy of supplying homes that are attractive to open market buyers, rather than simply building exclusively for those that need public housing.

Finally, we should be prepared to make better use of the 106 strategy when the housing market recovers. For all its flaws, it is a legitimate source of supply, and can also, when used well, be an invaluable vehicle for the creation of greater housing mix.

Nevertheless, even prior to the housing crash, 106 agreements were only applied to 14 per cent of new developments.[78] Now this proportion is set to plummet from an already low base. Thames Gateway is, once again, a prime example, as its developers are apparently seeking to renegotiate their existing 106 obligations, driving down the proportion of affordable and public housing.[79]

If we are to begin to get the full potential out of 106 agreements we need, first of all, to change the basic terms of the agreements. Instead of permitting Local Authorities to require a public housing component in developments of 15 units and above, we should *require* them to pursue 106 agreements in all developments that have more than 10 units. In (rare) cases where this would lead to an over-supply of public housing, the Local Authority would be required to satisfy an external body (see below) that its existing social provision was not only adequate, but also genuinely mixed.[80]

Moreover, local and regional authorities must be given, and required to use, greater powers in enforcing such agreements. Very often house builders try to drive down the public housing component of developments, seeking to satisfy the 106 requirement with affordable bought housing instead. Often this reflects genuine fears about financial viability, but it can also be driven by less legitimate concerns, either on the part of developers, or on the part of Local Authorities that want to restrict public housing for political reasons. Where this is the case, regional authorities must ensure that mix proportions reflect local housing need, and all regions should have the same power as the London Mayor to veto large developments that do not reflect balanced need. The threshold for using this power in London is currently on developments of 150 units and over. It should be reduced to at least 75.

In addition to the sticks of regulation, there must also be carrots for private developers in the form of impartial advice for smaller developers, helping them to plan for greater social provision in a way that is financially viable. To this end, an independent arbitration service should be established. Often the reluctance of private developers to

57

embrace larger volumes of public housing has reflected legitimate concerns about financial viability, and financial viability will vary regionally. A national planning framework must therefore reflect this and remain flexible, as well as having more teeth when needed. Experience suggests that many developers have in fact willingly provided a greater proportion of social units when they have had access to independent, expert advice, paid for by the Local Planning Authority. Once the process has become less adversarial developers have tended to become less defensive of their margins, and have often seen that a greater proportion of public housing is in fact commercially viable. Conversely, some Local Planning Authorities have felt themselves to be at a disadvantage when negotiating with large developers, who can sometimes approach the process aggressively. A national, independent advice and arbitration service should ease negotiations and could refer cases to the Homes and Communities Agency (HCA; which replaces the Housing Corporation) if necessary. But the presumption should be that this is part of the normal planning process in the first instance, and only a conflict resolution service in more difficult cases. The same agency could be responsible for ensuring that Local Authorities are meeting the obligations on mix (see above).

Ensuring supply is mixed

We have now seen how we might increase supply in a number of ways, including making better use of private-public partnerships. Nevertheless, we must be wary of repeating one of the most destructive mistakes of the past: the rush to volume at the expense of both quality and mix.

When supply picks up we need to ensure that the principles of successful mix, enumerated above, are met in practice. The HCA has a crucial role to play here. It must attach far more stringent conditions to the provision of Housing Grant, not just to specific developments, but to areas as well. This would mean that Local Authorities cannot just pick and choose which specific developments are planned and managed in accordance with the principles of mix. Local Authorities that do not meet these standards would be penalised in further rounds of Housing Grant.

Specifically, there needs to be vigilant monitoring of both pepper-potting and tenure blindness. 106 agreements have gained a good deal of notoriety precisely because the public housing component of a development is often in the darker recesses, overlooking the bins, in the least desirable parts of the estate. The result is to replicate the status divisions and labelling that mix is meant to counteract. The same approach must be applied to the provision of family homes in both the private and the social sector: if we are to have mixed areas and neighbourhoods we must remove the need for families to move on once they reach a certain age and size. At the same time, the HCA should be the vehicle used to replicate nationally the successful example of SAVE.

Threats to sustainable mix

The sad fact is that good practice, both in terms of mix and in terms of connection to infrastructure and services, is not in fact the norm. When mix is planned badly it will be difficult to attract a range of incomes, and those that do buy will either seek to exit as soon as possible, or will buy with the intention of becoming landlords rather than residents. Enumerated below are some of the obstacles to achieving mix, and some of the worst practices that must be stopped by legislation and robust policy.

At the very top of the list of threats, we should note, is the ruinous effect that the right to buy has had, and will continue to have, on the stability of mixed communities. The problem here is not that social tenants get to change tenure; it is that, once they do so, they almost invariably exit the area, and the new owner is very often a buy-to-let investor. No matter how well planned a development or area intervention is, if the social landlord loses control of a sufficient supply of stock, and is not allowed to replenish the stocks through sales receipts, it will not be able to discharge its role.

Second to this is the process by which the owner occupied tenure in fact becomes a rented sector. This can arise naturally enough through residents moving on and maintaining their flat as an investment, but where mix has failed it has often been through block buying of units by buy-to-let investors. Often this has involved commercial companies buying up flats and then letting them directly to Local Authorities who use them to meet emergency housing need. Instead of owner occupation we quickly arrive at precisely the phenomenon that mix was intended to address: the concentration of the neediest individuals in pockets of public housing.[81]

Thirdly, there is also a tendency for a majority of developers to cluster public housing units, either for ease of management or because they believe (falsely) that the lease-hold units will be hard to sell if they are not insulated from social tenants.

A fourth major risk comes from the practice of both private developers and the then Housing Corporation to concentrate almost exclusively on building flats and maisonettes rather than larger houses. Even if an area is attractive and popular across all tenures (as Greenwich Millennium Village is, for example) there will be a tendency for those who can to leave once their family reaches a certain age or size. This voluntary exit represents a significant risk to the popularity, stability and the mix of the area.

Finally, a fifth set of risks revolves around the failure to connect communities with proper infrastructure. Many of the developments (for example, Ebbsfleet and Barking Riverside) in the Thames Gateway Growth Area fall into this category. Even where the dwellings are well designed, they tend not to pass the 'pint of milk test': there are no commercial facilities, no entertainment opportunities, and, typically, very poor transport connections. In a rising market, some of these developments will indeed be commercially viable, but large clusters will have been bought by buy to let investors, and young professionals or key workers that do buy and move in invariably see it as a stepping stone to something better. And if they haven't already moved on, the lack of popular schools is likely to lead to exit once these households start families.

Regulation of tenure and buy to let

At the heart of all the risks faced by mixed communities is the risk of instability; of a loss of social balance arising from an excessive outflow of owners, or an excessive inflow of tenants (social or private). Mix typically fails where the intended balance of the community or neighbourhood is altered. There are two specific policies that we should pursue to counter some of these risks.

Paramount here is not only that social units remain social, thereby entailing a bar on the right to buy in mixed developments, but also that the private units remain owner-occupied. One way to achieve this is to structure tax on rentals in such a way that it discourages the transition of owner-occupied dwellings into the rented sector: rental revenues should be taxed in proportion to social cost. Rentals that alter the intended balance of planned mixed developments should be taxed at a higher rate to reflect the potential social cost of the change. This would apply to both commercial landlords and private landlords who have either left the development but retained the property as an investment, or to private landlords who have bought off the original owner with the intention of letting the property. The revenue raised should then be ring-fenced for either investment in new stock, or to pay into a capital fund that contributes to the management of the development over time. This should be directed at extra advisory services for all residents (though tailored to those with most need) and could include employment and training services.

We must also block another common route by which social balance is seriously disturbed. There has been a tendency for property companies to buy clusters of flats for private rental. Clearly this can alter the intended composition of ownership, and the clustering runs against the principles of pepper-potting. But the threat immediately becomes far more serious when we consider who these homes are rented out to: they are often rented en bloc by Local Authorities to house the homeless under their statutory duties.[82] In other words, large, concentrated blocks of housing are given over to the neediest, without any serious attempts at integration. The result is precisely the opposite of mix, both in terms of tenure and in the deeper sense that we have been concerned with throughout this pamphlet.

It would be wrong, and contrary to the deeper principles of mix, to prevent Local Authorities from using this option to house families in good communities. The simplest and most direct policy solution is therefore to restrict multiple purchases; buying in clusters of more than two should be banned.

Managing mix

It is clear, then, that successful mix requires active and ongoing management well after the planning stages. Furthermore, this management is not just about maintaining social balance. At the end of my analysis of the importance of mix, I entered a crucial caveat: we cannot expect housing mix to be a panacea for poverty. On its own, it is not enough to overcome the barriers that have locked many social housing tenants into poverty; and sometimes mix will prove impractical, at least in the short-term. In the latter case, it is vital that we seek other forms of institutional and social reconnection, and the best vehicle for doing so is through traditional housing management structures.

There are therefore two sets of policy areas that we need to address in relation to housing mix and management: the first concerns the role of management in making mix work, and the second concerns the role of management in improving the life-chances of residents where physical integration proves to be impractical. The former is discussed below; the latter is the topic of the next section of this chapter.

Let us start with the policies needed to make the management of mixed communities effective. The two key issues here are the need to finance quality management services, and the need to address the potential problems that could arise between different tenures. Many of the policies here are directly applicable to non-mixed communities.

All high-density developments need intensive management to maintain the quality of the stock and the public spaces, and this is especially the case in mixed developments, where tensions and bad management can lead to an exodus of the higher-income households.

The lesson is simply that proximity to services and institutions pays a considerable dividend in terms of services, quality of management and social capital.

Indeed, there is good evidence to suggest that estate-based management is cost effective in turning around difficult estates.[83] Active neighbourhood and estate management significantly improves the liveability of deprived areas, and has a positive impact in reducing stigma. Active management is also crucial in maintaining the stability of mixed communities, where there is potential for tension between tenures if public housing is perceived to be the source of antisocial behaviour.

Yet just at the same time that some of this evidence began to emerge, a very large number of Local Authorities began centralising their management structure through call centres – the exact opposite of the social and institutional connection that is desperately needed. In large part this has been in response to the Best Value Regime, which audits the performance of Local Authorities in terms of efficiency and value for money. So the regime must be reformed to reflect the social benefits of estate-based management.

Clearly, intensive management does come at a cost, and since the early 1990s service charges have not been claimable under Housing Benefit. The result is that public housing tenants struggle to pay the charges, and the social landlord may succumb to the temptation to reduce the level of service in order to keep charges down. This can lead to a situation in which (for example) the bins of social rented dwellings are collected less often, leading, for example, to the perception of antisocial behaviour. In order to prevent this, service charges should be claimable on Housing Benefit. Care obviously needs to be taken to ensure that 'services' are tightly circumscribed and confined to mainstream services if the financial burden on Housing Benefit is not to be excessive.

There is also scope for more radical changes in subsidy of service charges and management costs. Private rental and owner-occupied houses in mixed communities should cross-subsidise service charges for public housing. At present, this form of cross subsidy is not legally permissible, and there should be a statutory change to overturn this. But the extra revenue raised should be directed to general area improvements that improve the quality of life of all residents, which are not funded out of a general repairs and maintenance budget, and which are not part of core housing services. One possibility would be that funds raised through cross-subsidy could be spent on activities that promote cross-tenure interaction, such as an ongoing gardening or an allotment scheme that is jointly managed by all residents. The sums involved in this could be either small or relatively large, depending on context. The aim is to promote interaction rather than as a key means of redistribution.

In order to make this politically feasible, there would of course have to be incentives for the private households that would contribute more. A higher cross-subsidy would necessitate some form of government capital subsidy for leaseholders. This could come in the form of a capital subsidy from Housing Grant, selling the homes at marginally below market rate in order to compensate for the ongoing cost of higher service charges. The subsidy would be justified on the basis of the presumed social gain arising from the enhanced neighbourhood quality and the potential to generate social capital and interaction that benefits all residents, and which potentially has the elusive role model effect for workless households. An alternative source of compensation or incentive would be a council tax discount for the households that paid more in service charges.

There are also changes that must be made not just to the funding of management, but also to the structure. Most mixed developments currently have two management structures, with a Housing Association managing the public housing and a private company managing the other tenures. This can exacerbate the tensions that have sometimes arisen between tenures, with different standards of service and management; and it continues to segregate housing (and individuals) by type. A unitary management would be more efficient and would, moreover, be better placed to tap into the potential social gains arising from cross-tenure interaction.

A unitary management structure would also be better placed to tap into the social capital that a well-balanced tenure mix has the potential to create. Once again, planning for adequate family dwellings is crucial. There is ample evidence that children are a very powerful vehicle for social interaction across tenure.[84] Young children do not make tenure distinctions. Furthermore, the latest national evaluation of Sure Start (Children's Centres) found that in many instances it was playing a very positive role in generating an area's social capital, bringing parents together in a range of services that encompass but also extend beyond childcare.[85] Qualitative research has also found that Sure Start can facilitate genuine social interaction, and that it can generate important 'bridging' of social capital. This not only links disadvantaged households to services they had not previously accessed, but it has also led to a more general broadening of horizons and aspirations.[86]

Section 2 – Beyond mix: promoting reattachment to public services

The integration of our housing stock can clearly not happen overnight. Given the extent to which poverty has been concentrated in the residualised end of the public housing sector, it will not be practical to integrate all housing in the short-term. Moreover, one cannot expect mix by itself to have a magical effect on poverty even when it is successful. Management must not only actively manage for mix, it must manage for other forms of social reconnection to labour markets and welfare institutions – as well as to wider society. This is equally true of both mixed developments and areas where mix might not be possible.

65

We now have ample evidence to show that, in areas of concentrated poverty, active neighbourhood and estate-based management significantly improves the reputation of an area and the quality of life of its residents.[87] Neighbourhood Wardens, for example, have been a great success, and greater investment and, for instance, concierge presence in tower blocks has led to some dramatic improvements. There is also good evidence from the latest national evaluation of New Deal for Communities areas, which tells us that 'evidence of change at the area level is overwhelmingly positive'.[88]

But, as we have seen, it is striking that, in spite of this evidence, there has been a growing tendency for Local Authorities to centralise their housing management structures in order to meet the efficiency standards of central Government's Best Value regime. That standard of efficiency was originally intended to go beyond a narrow bean counting exercise: part of the point of the Best Value regime was that it would be used to assess wider social value too. Nevertheless, in practice there has been a marked tendency for Local Authorities to interpret in narrowly. The net result is almost the exact opposite of institutional and social connection: residents are increasingly served through remote call centres rather than housing officers intimately familiar with the needs of local residents.

Equally striking is the way in which 'housing' management has become narrowly circumscribed, with a remit that covers stock maintenance, rent and repairs, and allocations, but has far too infrequently extended to wider advisory services and support. These should encompass, in particular, advice and support with employment and training services, and confidence and capacity building initiatives aimed at helping individuals back into the labour market. It is only by extending the housing management remit in this way that we can build on the achievements of neighbourhood and estate-based management; taking it beyond an improvement in liveability, and allowing management to have an impact on the causes of poverty, rather than just on its symptoms.

There have in fact been two positive policy developments in this regard. Firstly, there have been an increasing number of 'Trailblazer' councils that have combined housing options advisory services with employment advice.[89] Secondly, the DWP has recently announced that Job Centre Plus services will be piloted in some Children's Centres (Sure Start).[90] This is precisely the kind of community centred and joined-up work between major departments (DWP, DLCG, DUIS) that is needed.

Yet, neither of these initiatives has been extended to housing management: the advisory service comes at the point of allocations and individual housing choices, but is not then extended beyond this once the individual has been housed; and Sure Start will not reach the many young male adults that have become totally detached from the labour market and who have not pursued training opportunities.

We therefore need clear incentives for Local Authorities and Registered Social Landlords to adopt a far more holistic approach. To this end, Housing Grant should come with the expectation that all public housing management should seek to replicate the innovations of some of the best Housing Associations, such as Notting Hill Housing Association in London, and offer comprehensive education, training and employment advisory services for their tenants. A key part of the advisory offer here, for example, must include information on Housing Benefit and how claimants may or may not be affected by the transition into work – an issue where uncertainty can often act as a barrier to work. (See 'Housing Benefit' section on page 70).

Case study of Notting Hill Housing

Notting Hill Housing Association has been one of the most innovative of a number of Housing Associations that are taking seriously the need to offer more than just basic housing management. All new tenants are interviewed not just about their housing needs, but also their employment needs as well. This advice and support is then ongoing throughout the duration of the tenancy, with the option to join a number of specific employment and training schemes. Of particular note is the award winning Construction Training Initiative, which secures training placements for tenants on public housing development sites, and supports them with training costs and college fees; ultimately leading to fully accredited qualifications. So far over 700 people have secured qualifications and construction jobs under the scheme. Further support is available to young tenants on the Fast Forward project. In this scheme tenants commit to a training and work plan in return for a short-hold tenancy and a comprehensive package of support for up to five years.

Moreover, the Notting Hill Housing offer is genuinely holistic, encompassing extensive advisory services designed to promote greater financial inclusion. This includes not only debt advice, but also expert advice on benefit entitlements. Notting Hill Housing also supported the establishment of the Hammersmith and Fulham Credit Union.

Reforms to Housing Benefit that resonate with this agenda

At present, Housing Benefit is administered by the Local Authority, whilst mainstream employment services are provided by the Department for Work and Pensions. In practice, this means that job seekers using the services of their local Job Centre Plus will receive assistance in finding a job, but will not receive advice on the implications for their Housing Benefit allowance. Fragmented services add needless layers of complexity and bureaucracy that can act as a barrier to exit from poverty.

These barriers of separation are also powerfully manifested in the very steep withdrawal rates of Housing Benefit: once an individual finds work, the loss of financial assistance means that for every pound they earn in work they will only actually be 35 pence better off. This can act as a disincentive to work participation and progression.[91] Moreover, when many individuals want to work despite this perverse incentive, the complexity of its administration can result in uncertainty, which can in turn act as a barrier to work.[92] Time and again the message from housing management practitioners is that it is not the steep withdrawal rate that discourages work, but the chronic instability and uncertainty that comes with work: very often the work is insecure and potentially short-term; and the benefits system is too slow to kick in again when it is needed. The result is often that the household must resort to ruinously expensive debt (and hence face a familiar spiral into poverty) or simply go without. Faced with this choice, some will choose not to come off benefits in the first place. Too often, an allocations system that filters people into concentrated areas of worklessness is accompanied by a benefits system seemingly designed to keep them there. The result is to 'segregate' public housing tenants at the bottom of the income spectrum.

Thus, the chronic instability that comes with movements in and out of work coupled with uncertainty surrounding the administration of Housing Benefit can at least appear to make complete withdrawal from the labour market the sensible option. This is why the holistic advisory-management services that Notting Hill and Hyde Housing have both developed are so crucial, and should be widely replicated right across the public housing sector, complementing but also sometimes supplanting Job Centre Plus where appropriate. And reform should not stop here: we also need to rethink the idea of a specific Housing Benefit and consider a more general Housing Cost Credit that brings all those receiving state assistance for housing costs into the same system. This central proposal is discussed below (See 'Rethinking Tenure Distinctions').

Moreover, very often those that have been detached from the labour market for a long time will not actively seek help, or attempt to access other services that can improve quality of life and offer routes out of poverty. For tenants that are 'hard to reach' there should be extensive outreach services, following the best practice of a number of New Deal for Community initiatives (such as EC1 in London's Islington area).

Case study of Hyde Housing

Hyde Housing is another Housing Association that has taken up the challenge of worklessness amongst its tenants. In Hyde's last comprehensive survey it found that 50 per cent of its tenants were unemployed. It knows that that 70 to 80 per cent of the new tenants it is taking on are workless. In one of its estates, Ocean Park in Bexley Heath, there is up to 90 per cent worklessness. Despite being relatively small for an estate (there are only

150 units), there is still a highly disproportionate number of Anti-Social Behaviour Orders on Ocean Park. Though this is an extreme example, the more general problem of worklessness ranges across their housing stock, and is not unique to city estates. The unemployment levels of their tenants in Kent, for example, is four times the local average.

Hyde is actively engaging with the challenges thrown up by such high concentrations of worklessness. Across all their housing stock (including the more dispersed housing in rural areas) all new tenants are now offered access to a personal advice service to support them into work or training. Crucially, Hyde has also recently adopted a very active outreach programme in which dedicated case-workers conduct door to door visits (even in isolated areas) to offer services and support to all tenants, referring them to further advice and opportunities as appropriate. As part of a holistic approach to housing need, this can include referral to debt advisory services as well. In the last eight months, just one advisor, covering both rural and urban Kent, has seen 91 residents, supported 15 into training, seven into volunteering, and ten into quality work.

Case study challenges (and policy needs)

The conversion rate of Hyde's outreach programme is impressive. So too is Notting Hill Housing's Construction Training Initiative. But there are two key constraints in their ability to do more. The first is financial: these important schemes are funded by the Housing Associations themselves, and have typically been cross-subsidised by sales in the open market. In the present climate this source of finance is clearly under severe threat. But it has never been assured in the good times either; funding for these schemes is a corporate option rather than an obligation, and external sources of funding (from Regional Development Agencies) tend to be bureaucratic, sluggish and uncertain.

These financial and organisational concerns have meant that many Housing Associations have not followed suit. The second key constraint is on the degree to which Hyde and Notting Hill Housing can influence the social mix on the estates that they manage. Virtually 100 per cent of the allocations on these estates are dictated by the Local Authority, who invariably take the top slice of those at the top of the housing waiting list. The result is the exact opposite of mix: concentration and the intractable problems that come with the worst estates of our housing world.

We therefore need two key policy responses to the constraints faced by active and innovative Housing Associations.

■ **Housing Associations should be given direct control over 50 per cent of lettings allocations.**
This is essential for social and income mix in existing public housing stock, and it frees Housing Associations to manage in a holistic way without facing the insurmountable challenges presented by such dense concentrations of social need found in some estates.

■ **Holistic services should be funded from mainstream sources, based on a per unit formula.**
For example, 1 per cent of all Housing Grant awards could be ring-fenced to fund a dedicated outreach capacity for the Housing Association in receipt of the Grant. Other funding formulae might include a system in which funds raised by Housing Associations are automatically matched by Housing Grant (up to a specified limit).

Section 3 – Rethinking tenure distinctions

Earlier in this Chapter I argued for building tenure blind and pepper-potted public housing. The key message here was that, in doing so, we can hope to break the vicious circle of labelling and separation that has been so central to the history of public housing in England. Nevertheless, there was also the promise that the analysis of mix I have provided could lead to more radical conclusions, and to offer a route in which we do not just disguise tenure differences, but break down the tenure distinction itself. In the following section I make good that promise and outline two ways in which policy should be used to break down some of the deepest institutional and social assumptions about the relationship between public and privately owned housing.

The first is gearing policy towards an expansion of shared ownership, including reform of the 'right to buy' and a new 'right to sell'. The second is an integration of the different schemes that currently exist to provide help with housing costs into a universal progressive benefit.

Promoting shared ownership

The concept of shared ownership has the potential to introduce a degree of universalism into tenure classification and property ownership, breaking down the polarisation between outright ownership and non-ownership, reducing the status division between tenures and preventing asset exclusion. Clearly in the current financial crisis, encouraging people to enter a falling market is not a good idea in the short term. Yet in the longer term, shared ownership is a means of offering some of the advantages of subsidised home-ownership, without reinforcing the cultural belief that this is somehow a morally superior form of tenure.

But, thus far, shared ownership has not taken off. Until very recently the shared ownership model has literally meant that the occupier owns a share of the home whilst a Housing Association owns the rest. The occupier takes out a mortgage on the part that they own, and pays rent to the Housing Association for the percentage that they own. This in fact introduces a degree of complexity to a system that has been poorly understood and can be off-putting. More importantly, the rental share can often be so high (as a reflection of local market rates, albeit at a subsidised level) that the overall cost to the occupier defeats the purpose.

Thus, a key failing with shared ownership is that there have been no controls on the rent that the occupier pays on the part of the home that they do not own. In practice, where this rent level is set by the local market rent, the more desirable areas can still be prohibitively expensive, which squeezes out lower income households and runs counter to the spirit of a mixed housing policy. A system of rent controls is therefore needed, set by reference to the Local Authority average, which brings the more popular areas into reach.

There has, to be fair, been a good deal of variety in the different schemes on offer, and I cannot enter into a case-by-case appraisal here. But it remains true that it has not caught the popular imagination. It is difficult not conclude that much of this has to do not just with the complexity of existing schemes, but also the variety itself: whilst the great range of occupier ownership on offer (from as little as 5 percent up to 75 per cent) seems laudable at first sight, the bottom end of this scale seriously undermines the asset opportunity that it is (in large part) intended to create. Furthermore, all too often the quality of intermediate housing has been poor, and therefore does not offer a good investment.

In response to this we need to increase the household equity share to 50 per cent, and offer far better guidance on the quality of their investment when individuals consider taking this step. One way of achieving this would be to set up a national scheme in which intermediate buyers were given a flat rate fee to pay a reputable estate agent to offer a realistic valuation of the property and its future market prospects.

There are in fact signs that some of the key reasons behind the failure of this shared ownership to take off could be overcome by the latest thinking in shared ownership. The Government's new HomeBuy Direct scheme operates on a different funding model and, strictly speaking, is a *shared equity* rather than a *shared ownership* scheme. This distinction brings with it the important feature of HomeBuy that the occupier does not pay rent on the remaining share. Instead, either the government or a private developer (the two alternative sponsors of shared equity) realises the value of their investment when the property is sold.

Thus far, the early signals are positive: Barratt Homes, for example, is pushing the scheme with enthusiasm, and have already had 20,000 registrations of interest.[93] Nevertheless, two key facts remain. If shared ownership, in the form of shared equity, is to be a genuine vehicle of opportunity we must still exercise vigilance in ensuring that the asset on offer is, firstly, a high quality home that would be attractive on the open market, and, secondly, that the equity share of the occupier is not so diluted that it amounts to mere tokenism; a genuflection to the ideological gods of ownership, but in practice no more. If we on the left are to seriously engage in asset equality, we must do so with real meaning and purpose.

Reassessing the right to buy

As we saw in Chapter 2, the right to buy has been one of the most pernicious forces that has driven the processes of residualisation. It has greatly reduced the stock of quality public housing and has led to the increasing concentration of poverty in the public housing that remains. In part this was due to the great financial restrictions that were placed on Local Authorities when their stock was sold, with the great bulk of the receipts from sales going into paying down debt rather than reinvesting in public housing. But it was also part and parcel of the broader ideology of the 'property owning democracy', a political movement that told us all that we were not full citizens unless we were home-owners.

The net result has been toxic: the physical and social separation of the public housing sector from the rest of society. Should we then follow the lead of the Scottish National Party and suspend the right to buy? There is a strong case to be made that we should indeed follow this lead, and over the course of the Labour Government there has been a steep reduction in the discount offered to potential buyers (now down to a maximum of 50 per cent from a peak of 70 per cent in 1989) and the length of tenancy required prior to buying has increased to five years, from a low of two.

But it would be foolish to think that we could now just abandon the right to buy and wait for a reversal of the destruction it has wrought. For a start, it has had a positive impact on the social mobility of many (but not all) of the 1.7 million households that have exercised the right over the past twenty eight years. And, of course, the aspiration of home ownership is entirely legitimate. Besides, it would be enormously naïve to think that the aspiration of ownership, with all the political connotations that are tied up with it, will simply wither away; even as we face possibly the most extraordinary housing crash that we have seen for generations – the bursting of a bubble that is every bit as ideological as it is economic. The problem is that the combined impact of exit and residualisation has often had profoundly negative side effects; both for those that can't exit, and, more broadly, for the perceived value of social housing as a public good.

So a two-pronged policy approach is required: better public housing, and far more of it; but also a mechanism whereby the political (and personal) aspiration for ownership can be met – without itself undermining the status and value of public housing as a public good. Ownership must not lead to separation.

Where does this leave the right to buy? Clearly, an active policy of shared ownership (including purchasing the property in full) presupposes that there is some kind of *a* right to buy; it is a right to subsidy and assistance in the housing market. Nevertheless, this does not mean that it should embody the same rights as the politically charged version of right to buy that we saw in the 1980s.

Quite simply, *a* right to buy *a* home should not mean that tenants should have a right to take public housing stock with them if and when they choose to leave the tenure. This is of the utmost importance where public housing has been built in desirable areas, or with the specific aim of mixed income and tenure. Where ownership is subsidised, the presumption should be that the household moves to their new home, just as those living in the private sector do. Leaving the public housing tenure must *not* mean that the stock is automatically taken with it. Thus, the current right to buy mechanism needs to be reformed and the structure of subsidised exit abolished.

75

A 'right to sell'

A reformed right to buy should be complemented by the introduction of a flexible option to sell, in which households are given the option of transferring some or all of their equity to their Local Authority, thereby reducing mortgage payments to a manageable level. An option to sell could be exercised, for example, if households experience a financial shock through ill health or redundancy, and this would allow them to stay in their own home, until they are able to increase their equity should they wish. Any uplift in the value of the property will be shared with the Local Authority, and should be ring-fenced to be invested in public housing.

Such a measure would not only go beyond current emergency measures of support, such as support for mortgage interest or government-backed mortgage payment 'holidays'. Specifically, it would go significantly beyond the very limited, and highly targeted, form of an option to sell that is currently on offer.[94] By introducing a more general right to apply for 'reverse staircasing', a more universal and mainstream approach (available not just in times of economic crisis) would blur a moralised distinction between owning and renting that labels public housing tenants as lesser citizens than owners. Whereas right to buy consciously created social and spatial distance between tenures and greatly contributed to the process of residualisation, an option to sell would reconnect citizens to the welfare system as a positive protective mechanism. And, crucially, it can be a direct vehicle of housing mix when the properties concerned are in areas that have a relatively low proportion of public housing.

Of course, the option we are presenting here is not a 'right' as such. Such a right would be both financially and administratively unrealistic, and open to abuse even if it could be made to work. This is why in policy terms I have presented it as an option rather than a right. But it is still an expression of a broader social right to housing assistance and protection for all members of our society, not just for those in a highly residualised and targeted system of public housing. As such, an option to sell is indeed to be seen as a direct practical and principled response to the shortcomings of the right to buy. In political and moral terms, a right to sell is just that: as much a 'right' as the right to buy.

A universal housing cost credit

We have seen how shared ownership blurs the distinction between ownership and rental status by introducing gradation into the system. This helps to break down the alienating, binary distinction between the public and the private in housing provision, and so helps lessen the temptation to see public housing as a sign of stigma, marking off a whole category of citizens as somehow socially inferior. But far more is needed, and there is scope for more radical action here. We need to do more than blur the distinction between ownership and public housing that can come with the practice of shared ownership. We also need broader ways to address the perception that public housing is only a targeted good for the poor. The current system of Housing Benefit plays into this perception at a deeper level, as its administration necessarily relies on the kind of institutional and administrative classifications that inadvertently help create the popular perception that public housing tenants form their own separate category of (second-class) citizens. The more radical step I am proposing here is, therefore, to scrap Housing Benefit as a system targeted only at the poor. Instead it should be replaced with a universal Housing Cost Credit, which would operate on the same principles as the Tax Credit system currently does.

Here I provide only a simple explication of the principle of a Housing Cost Credit. Tax credits such as the Working Tax Credit and the Child Tax Credit currently provide for different needs within the same system, such as providing additional money for disabled people through the Working Tax Credit (in addition to the more general earnings top ups). In the same way, a Housing Cost Credit would bring together – within a single system – the different elements of financial assistance with housing costs currently available, such as support for mortgage interest and Housing Benefit. Furthermore, through a more gradual taper, such a credit would extend support further up the income spectrum than Housing Benefit usually reaches, thereby offering support to a wider range of households (such as lower-middle income households struggling with mortgage interest).

Public housing tenants – and those currently paying for private accommodation out of Housing Benefit – would still receive direct financial assistance from the Local Authority to meet their housing costs. But, importantly, they would be part of the same universal system; there would cease to be a clear institutional (and all too easily moralised) distinction between public and private housing's respective relationships with the state.

A case in point is the Support for Mortgage Interest offered to homeowners now struggling with their mortgage repayments. Such help is the right and proper response, but it comes under an entirely different scheme from Housing Benefit; when in principle there is no normatively relevant distinction between the two forms of assistance. So, in continuing to distinguish different schemes of support for different categories of tenure (and, implicitly, different income groups), the government is missing an important opportunity to integrate all housing help into a universal progressive benefit; and to thereby send out an important institutional and political message about the legitimacy of both the welfare state and, more specifically, the tenure of public housing. It would therefore be far better to encompass assistance for public housing and for homeowners in a single credit system to help with housing costs – of which rent and mortgage interest would be different elements – which would extend much higher up the income spectrum, with assistance progressively tapering away at the top.

As well as eliminating the current steep withdrawal of Housing Benefit, which imposes high marginal effective tax rates, such a system could give more help to low and middle income households with their housing costs, leaving it as open whether or not they make best use of this assistance through social or private renting or steps to home ownership. Of course, this more generous progressive universalism comes at a cost. One quite direct way of paying for this would be to remove the exemption from capital gains tax on principal primary residences (which is currently worth some £16 billion a year) – something that could perhaps offset the potentially inflationary impact on the housing market of offering more help with housing costs to middle-income households.

And indirectly, over time, if the argument of this pamphlet is correct, the unifying spirit of a progressive universalism will gradually create the political and social climate in which a properly funded state system of public housing no longer seems a pipedream. A tall order perhaps, but we should not forget that housing institutions can be the vehicle of deep political change. We saw this all too clearly under Thatcher. It is now time for the left's own historical moment in housing: a deep institutional and value-based response to the ideology of citizenship as independence that came with the right to buy.

5 | Conclusion

To some on the left, the arguments and recommendations of this pamphlet will undoubtedly fail to persuade. Poverty and inequality, for these critics, boils down to a simple problem of income poverty. Forget all the talk of 'place', community and mix, they will say. These are just a distraction from the fight against the economic injustices that are the causes of poverty.

I do not see the ideal of mixed communities (and mix in the deeper sense, across our national stock) as any kind of silver bullet. Yet it is an immensely important part of the story that we need to tell about how we, as a society, have reached such levels of poverty and inequality over the last 30 years. We neglect this lesson at our peril.

The sceptics are in fact profoundly wrong about the importance of mix. I do not simply mean here that concentrations of poverty in housing estates are a cause as well as a symptom of poverty (though this remains an under-recognised and crucial conclusion).

The deeper lesson is that welfare for the poor quickly becomes poor welfare. A narrowly targeted system undermines public support for welfare distribution, and ultimately erodes the political legitimacy of the welfare state – and with it the capacity for the redistribution needed to address hard income poverty. Indeed, the highly targeted and resid-ualised provision of public housing in the UK clearly exemplifies this pernicious process: the more it has been targeted, the more the tenure –and the tenants - have been stigmatised.

Nothing ultimately does more to sap the public and political will to make the social and economic adjustments that a more just society requires.

The legitimacy and popularity of welfare institutions is moret han about 'argument'. The beliefs and attitudes that support the legitimacy of the welfare state are themselves the product of the way it is structured. Ironically, Thatcher instinctively understood this power of institutions to shape attitudes. This is why the 'right to buy' legislation fell so neatly into the parameters of Thatcherite ideology: it both reflected and sustained that structure of beliefs and social expectations. The difference, of course, is that the institutions she used to drive her politics were those of the market; and even when it was really the hand of the state doing the work (as it was in the massive discounts on council homes) it was the idea of the market that was doing the normative and strategic work.

What the left really needs is not more argument, but its own institutional corrective to the legacy of the Thatcherite era. For far too long we have seen public housing as just bricks and mortar; a material resource to be distributed fairly. What we have failed to really see is the way in which a progressive vision of public housing, based on the deeper values of mix articulated in this pamphlet, can and should be a vehicle for the values of the left. That is the aim of the core policy directions advocated here: housing and income mix in the broadest sense, and system of state housing assistance (the Housing Cost Credit) that brings us all into one institutional system of progressive universalism.

Both sets of policies are intended, over time, to embed in our society the broad acceptance of our interdependence as equal citizens; rather than a society built upon the premise that turning to the state for assistance is a mark of a second class citizen. Only once we realise this interdependence as a social fact will public housing attain the status and recognition it deserves as one of our most important and valuable public goods – part of the fabric of a just society.

In the Mix

Case studies
What successful mix looks like

The Greenwich Millennium Village (GMV)

GMV is an 'urban village', built as part of the Government's Millennium Communities Programme, and the first residents moved in during 2000. In 2004 50 per cent of the residents were 'very satisfied', and a majority of residents held positive attitudes towards the mix. Over 75 per cent of parents rated it very highly as a place to bring up children.[95]

GMV now has approximately 30 per cent public housing tenants, with the remainder being comprised of a mix of owners and (as a minority in the overall mix) private renters. The developer also took a conscious decision not to offer discounts to multiple purchasers, so it has not merely become a buy to let opportunity for investors, and GMV is a stable and popular community: those who live there typically put down roots, and the social mix is not disrupted by the buy-to-let market. The development is also genuinely 'tenure blind' and pepper-potted: there are no visible signs that a dwelling is public housing, and the public housing units are not clustered together.

Infrastructure has been important too. Not only are the homes in GMV of high quality, the public space is well-designed and well-serviced by numerous transport links and a very popular primary school. Crucially, this infrastructure was in place *before* the first residents moved in.

Nevertheless, GMV is by no means perfect. Recently there has been some controversy over the inability of public housing tenants to pay the high levels of service charges that are needed to manage a quality mixed development successfully; and that management has a tendency (common to a majority of mixed developments) to be fragmented between the private and social homes. Moreover, a potential threat to the future sustainability of GMV arises because of a lack of private houses rather than flats or maisonettes (where will these families go when they need more space?). There are also concerns about the quality of the nearest secondary school. Many homeowners thought it likely that they would move on when these issues became pressing.[96]

New Earswick, York

Originally built by Joseph Rowntree to house both his factory workers and the local population, the village contained a wide range of incomes (though not tenure) and was consciously designed to be a balanced community. By the 1980s – with the right to buy – the balance had been upset by the exit of large numbers of the higher income households. Typically, these residents were replaced by priority households on the council's waiting list, and the 'model' village had become a model of residualisation and stigma. Though tenants did not have the right to buy, the Joseph Rowntree Housing Trust has operated an alternative scheme whereby better off tenants were given financial assistance to buy elsewhere and move away from the village.

Their response, in 1997, was to initiate SAVE: Selling Alternate Vacants on Estates.[97] The explicit aim was to rebalance the community by selling 50 per cent of all properties that became vacant. The receipt from sales was to be ploughed back into building more public housing stock, thereby maintaining supply and balance. Top of the list of properties up for sale were the least popular homes and locations, as the SAVE scheme was designed so as not to replicate a social hierarchy in which the least independent are left with the housing of last resort. There was also concern that buy-to-let investors would crowd in and, in effect, turn the area into a rented slum area. This was prevented by strict conditions in the leaseholds of the sold properties. The properties have not been difficult to sell on the open market. Quite the opposite: the Village is a popular neighbourhood with market prices that match or outperform the area.[98] What is left is a viable, mixed community that has shed the stigma and much of the disadvantage previously associated with it. An increasing number of Local Authorities are adopting this approach, typically for the pragmatic reason that the costs of maintaining the buildings they are selling can be very high, but invariably with the later recognition that SAVE and mix has also had a very positive impact on the reputation of the neighbourhood.

Bournville Village Trust (BVT).[99]

Bournville Village Trust area is in one respect strikingly different to New Earswick: it was never broken, and it does not need to be fixed. Nor does it have, unlike, the Greenwich Millennium Village, the flavour of a grand social experiment. It is simply a balanced community that, albeit with some social problems, has always worked. Now a large suburb of Birmingham rather than just the original model village of the Nineteenth Century, the BVT in fact manages approximately 8000 properties, 40 per cent of which are social rented. Most of the rest are owned. The social tenants, when compared with public housing tenants nationally, have very high satisfaction rates with the quality of home, area and management. Whereas 64 per cent of Bournville residents describe their neighbourhood as 'pleasant', only 36 per cent of public housing tenants nationally do. 70 per cent of all residents (including owners) were 'very satisfied' with the area.[100] Similarly positive results emerge across a wide range of indicators, with far lower rates of anti-social behaviour being particularly significant.

Why is this so? Good connection to labour markets is one reason. A significant number of the residents are still employed by the Bournville chocolate factory, and the area is well connected to local labour markets more generally, and it does not exhibit the same concentrations of worklessness that disfigure other public housing areas. More generally, BVT itself attributes its success to high quality build and architecture; an activist management that involves the community; and an imaginative and coherent overall planning framework.

But there is one key point from a recent evaluation that really stands out:

> "In analysing the impact of housing mix in Bournville, however, it is important to acknowledge a major factor which has insulated the Trust, and the social rented sector associated with it, from the changes which have affected public housing more generally. Bournville Village Trust, as a charitable organisation, *has not been obliged to sell properties under the right to buy* . The extent to which the social rented sector remains intact in an attractive, high demand area is therefore unusual." (Emphasis added).[101]

Principles of good mix

From these case studies we can abstract the following ingredients of successful mix, with neighbourhoods that are popular areas of choice, and which continue to maintain a stable social mix over time:

- Tenure mix is a proxy for income mix, with a range of incomes in the community;
- Homes within the community are attractive and of high quality, and attract genuine open market interest;
- The design is such that the homes are 'tenure blind': it is not possible to tell by appearance the status of the resident;
- Tenure blindness works best where different tenures are thoroughly integrated and 'pepper-potted';
- The mixed community must be actively managed, both in terms of maintaining the mix, and in terms of reducing tensions that may arise between tenures;
- The community needs to be stable: the income mix must not be allowed to radically alter over time. There must be some meaningful perpetuity of tenure – public housing is to remain public housing, or the stock must be replenished;

■ The wider space in which the homes are embedded is attractive, safe and suitable for children. Sustainable mix needs to be family friendly.

It should be clear that all these principles apply to public housing across the board, and to all neighbourhoods. But where mix is not possible, or where it is not practical to introduce mix into an existing mono-tenure area, the following principles of external reconnection are also particularly important. They are crucial to both the success of mixed communities, and that of other housing developments where mix itself proves to be impractical.

■ There must be good infrastructure and services that connect all residents to labour markets, consumer markets, and quality public services;
■ Connection to good quality schools is vital;
■ Sufficient transport connections are crucial.

In the Mix

References

1   Anuerin Bevan, 1949, quoted in Hills (2007:86)

2   Planning Policy Statement 3 (PPS3): Housing, DCLG, 2006

3   N Buck, 'Identifying area effects on social exclusion', Urban Studies, 38, 200 [DATE].

4   J. Blasius, J. Friedrichs, G. Glaster, 'Introduction: frontiers of quantifying neighbourhood effects', Housing Studies, 25(5), 2007.

5   CSDH (2008). Closing the gap in a generation: health equity through action on the social determinants of health. Final Report of the Commission on Social Determinants of Health.Geneva, World Health Organization p32.

6   Feinstein et al, The public value of social housing: a longitudinal analysis of the relationship between housing and life chances, p 9.

7   John Hills, Ends and Means: The Future Roles of Social Housing in England, CASE report 34, 2007, p.5.

8   Singleton et al., Psychiatric Morbidity Survey among Adults Living in Private Households, cited in Royal College of Psychiatrists, Mental Health and Work, 6.

9   David Fone et al., "Places, people and mental health: A multi-level analysis of economic inactivity", SocialScience & Medicine 64 (2007), 633.

10   Leon Feinstein, Ruth Lupton, Cathie Hammond, Tamjid Mujaba, Emma Salter and Annik Sorhaindo, The public value of social housing: a longitudinal analysis of the relationship between housing and life chances, The Smith Institute, 2008.

11   Feinstein et al

12   John Hills, Inequality and the State, Oxford University Press, 2004, pp. 14-16.

13   The scale of advantage / disadvantage referred to here is an index calculated on the basis of family background characteristics.

Fienstein et al, The public value of social housing, pp 32-33.

14   This pamphlet does not deal with the many issues surrounding life-chances and the private rental market. This is, of course, a matter of regret, as there is a great need for a properly regulated, quality private rental sector in the UK Nevertheless, it is simply not possible to address all housing issues in the scope of one pamphlet. And it remains the case that it is public housing, not private rented, that most displays the characteristics of a tenure of disadvantage in the emerging evidence that we have. It is the need to address this is ultimately the more pressing need for those concerned with social justice.

15   Danny Dorling, Jan Rigby, Ben Wheeler, Dimitris Ballas, Bethan Thomas, Eldin Fahmy, Dave Gordon and Ruth Lupton, Poverty and wealth across Britain 1968 to 2005, Joseph Rowntree Foundation, Findings, 2007.

16   Dorling, D., Rigby, J., Wheeler, B., Ballas, D., Thomas, B., Fahmy, E., Gordon, D. and Lupton, R. (2007), Poverty, wealth and place in Britain, 1968 to 2005, Bristol: The Policy Press, p. 31.

17   Hills, Ends and Means, p 2.

18   Alan Murie, Moving Homes: the Housing Corporation 1964-2008,Politicos, 2008, p, 243.

19   An excellent discussion of this is to be found in Sarah Wise's study of the workhouse and slums of the Eastend of the late Victorian period (The Blackest Streets: The Life and Death of a Victorian Slum, Bodley Head, 2008).

20   Anne Power and John Houghton, Jigsaw Cities; Big places, small places ,Policy Press, 2007 p 47

21   P, Collison, The Cutteslowe Walls: A Study in Social Class, Faber and Faber, London, 1963

22   Power and Houghton, Jigsaw Cities, p 50.

23   Cited in Lynsey Hanley, Estates; An Intimate History, Granta, 2007, p 77

24   Jim Bennett with David Hetherington, Max Nathan and Chris Urwin , Would You Live Here? Making the Growth Areas communities of choice , Institute of Public Policy Research, 2006, p 22

25   Rodney Lowe, The Welfare State in Britain Since 1945, Palgrave, 2005, p, 258.

26   Nicholas Timmins, The Five Giants: A Biography of the Welfare State, Harper Collins, 2001, p 184

27   Timmins, The Five Giants, p 184

28   Timmins, The Five Giants, p, 184

29   Power and Houghton, Jigsaw Cities, p, 63

30   Timmins, The Five Giants, p 233.

31   Power and Houghton, Jigsaw Cities p 60

32   Alison Ravetz, Council Housing and Culture: The History of a Social Experiment, Routledge, 2001, p, 199.

33   Howard Glennerster, British Social Policy: 1945 to the present, Blackwell, 2007, p 188.

34   John Campbell, Margaret Thatcher, Volume Two: The Iron Lady, Jonathan Cape, 2003, p 234.

35   For example, on the comparatively poor performance of the US, UK and Ireland on child poverty, see UNICEF (2007) Child poverty in perspective: An overview of child well-being in rich countries. Innocenti Report Card 7, Innocenti Research Centre: Florence.

36   See, for example, Miller, D. (1999) Principles of Social Justice. Oxford: Oxford University Press.

37   Tajfel, H. & Turner, J. C. (1986) 'The social identity theory of intergroup behavior', in S. Worchel and L. W. Austin (eds.), Psychology of Intergroup Relations. Chicago: Nelson-Hall.

38   Heatherton, T.F., Kleck, R.E., Hebl, M.R. & Hull, J.G. (eds.) (2000) The Social Psychology of Stigma. New York: Guilford Press

39   Opotow, S. (1990) 'Moral exclusion and injustice: an introduction' Journal of Social Issues 46(1), p.1-20; Montada, L. & Schneider, A. (1989) 'Justice and emotional reactions to the

disadvantaged' Social Justice Research, 3, p.313-344.

40   Brewer, M. B., & Kramer, R. M. (1986) 'Choice behavior in social dilemmas: Effects of social identity, group size and decision framing' Journal of Personality and Social Psychology, 3, p.543-549.

41   van Oorschot, W. (2000) 'Who should get what, and why? On deservingness criteria and the conditionality of solidarity among the public' Policy and Politics 28, p.33-48.

42   DWP (2006) A new deal for welfare: empowering people to work. London: DWP; DWP (2008) No one written off: reforming welfare to reward responsibility London: DWP

43   Liz Richardson, Where should Housing Policy go Next?, New Local Government Network, 2007, p, 9.

44   Power and Houghton. Jigsaw Cities, p 61.

45   National Consumer Council, Why do the poor pay more...or get less?, 2004.

46   Terry Brooks and Matt Fellowes, The High Price of Being Poor in Kentucky, The Brookings Institute, 2007.

47   New Deal for Communities: A Synthesis of New Programme Wide Evidence: 2006-07, NDC National Evaluation Phase 2, Research Report 39, p, 6, DCLG.

48   Competition Commission, Home Credit Market Investigation, 2006.

49   Institute of Fiscal Studies, Press Release, January 24th, 2007.

50   Jane Phipps and Francesca Hopwood Road, Deeper in debt: the profile of CAB clients, Citizens Advice Bureau, 2006; Elaine Kempson, Over-indebtedness in Britain: A report to the Department of Trade and Industry, 2002.

51   Peter Kemp, 'Housing Benefit and public housing in England', The future of public housing, Shelter, 2008, p 61.

52   DWP (2006) A new deal for welfare: empowering people to work. London: DWP

53   Del Roy Fletcher, Tony Gore, Kesia Reeve and David Robinson, Public housing and worklessness: Key policy messages,

Department for Work and Pensions, Research Report No 482.

54   Jo Dean and Annette Hastings, Challenging images: Housing estates, stigma and regeneration, p 14.

55   And, recalling the high incidence of mental health problems amongst social tenants outlined in Chapter 1, it is also worth noting that psychological studies of stigma have highlighted the associated stress and anxiety of those who undergo stigmatisation as possible sources of mental health problems.

56   The full question is as follows: "The Government has suggested that, instead of having stand-alone social housing estates, new social housing should be mixed in with private housing, so that private owners and council tenants can be neighbours. Do you think this is a good idea or a bad idea?"

57   See, for example, Anne E Green and Richard J White, Attachment to place: Social networks, mobility and prospects of young people, Joseph Rowntree Foundation, 2007.

58   Keith Kintrea, 'Social Housing and Spatial Segregation', The Future of Social Housing, ed, Suzanne Fitzpatrick and Mark Stephens, Shelter, 2008.

59   Private interview.

60   Allen, C., Camina, M., Casey, R., Coward, S. and Wood, M. (2006) Mixed tenure twenty years on: Nothing out of the ordinary. Joseph Rowntree Foundation

61   See, for example, Paul Cheshire, Are mixed communities the answer to segregation and poverty?. JRF, 2007.

62   Chris Allen, Margaret Camina, Rionach Casey, Sarah Coward and Martin Wood, Mixed Tenure Twenty Years On – Nothing Out of the Ordinary, JRF, CIH, 2005.

63   Chris Holmes, Mixed communities: success and sustainability, JRF, 2006.

64   Graham Martin and Judi Watkinson, Rebalancing communities Introducing mixed incomes into existing rented housing estates, JRF, 2003, p 7.

65   Rob Rowlands, Alan Murie and Andrew Tice, More than tenure mix: Developer and purchaser attitudes to new housing estate, JRF, 2006.

66   Rob Rowlands, Alan Murie and Andrew Tice, More than tenure mix: Developer and purchaser attitudes to new housing estates, JRF, 2006. pp, 23-24.

67   Graham Martin and Judi Watkinson, Rebalancing communities Introducing mixed incomes into existing rented housing estates, 2008.

68   Rebecca Tunstall and Alex Fenton, In the Mix, a review of mixed income, mixed tenure and mixed communities: what do we know? Housing Corporation, English Partnerships and the Joseph Rowntree Foundation, 2006, p, 15.

69   Ruth Lupton, '"Neighbourhood Effects": Can we measure them and dies it matter?', London School of Economics, CASE Paper 73, 2003.

70   Sako Musterd and Roger Andersson, 'Employment, Social Mobility and Neighbourhood Effects: The Case of Sweden', International Journal of Urban and Regional Research, Volume, 30.1, March 2006.

71   Åslund O., Östh, J. & Zenou Y. 2007 'How important is access to jobs? Old question- improved answer.in Home, Job and Space, (ed) John Östh. Geografiska regionstudier nr 72. Kulturgeografiska institutionen, Uppsala Universitet

72   Musterd and Andersson, 'Employment, Social Mobility and Neighbourhood Effects', p 127.

73   Ibid.

74   Musterd S. Andersson R. Galster G, Kauppinen T, (2007) 'What Mix Matters? Exploring the Relatioshiops between Individuals' Incomes and Different Measures of their Neighbourhood Context', Housing Studies Vol. 22 No. 5, 637-660

75   Ibid, p 656.

76   Homes for the Future: More Affordable, More Sustainable,

94

DCLG, 2007, p 72.

77   'New freedoms to increase council house building', DCLG press release, Wednesday 21st, January, 2009.

78   The Community Infrastructure Levy. DCLG, 2008.

79   'Gateway developers cut low cost homes', Inside Housing, Wednesday, 11 March, 2009.

80   There is of course a familiar counter-argument to placing such a requirement on Local Authorities. It is, simply, that such measures could and would delay the development of much needed public housing. This is a pressing objection, particularly in the current economic climate, with the devastating impact if has had on the rate building starts and completions across the housing sector. But we have been here before. The need for a massive programme of public housing was never more acute than in the post-war period. Yet it was the very sense of urgency that this need created that was, in a vitally important sense, part of the problem rather than the solution. For, as we saw in Chapter 2, it was the great rush to volume of the post-war period that perhaps did most to undermine Bevan's vision of quality and social mix. The great danger today is that we will repeat that mistake and increase supply only in the short-term, at the price of further devaluing public housing in the longer-term. To put it simply, we need the will and patience – difficult though it is – to resist these calls for 'development now' unless we can be sure that it is the *right* type of development.

81   Tunstall and Fenton, In the Mix, A review of mixed income, mixed tenure and mixed communities, p, 41.

82   Ibid.

83   Rebecca Tunstall and Alice Coulter, Twenty-five years on Twenty Estates: turning the tide?. JRF, 2006. CABE on cost analysis

84   See, for example, E Silverman, Ruth Lupton and Alex Fenton, A Good Place for Children? Attracting and retaining families in inner urban mixed income communities, JRF, 2005.

85   Fiona Williams and Harriet Churchill, Empowering Parents in Sure Start Local Programmes National Evaluation of Sure Start (NESS) Institute for the Study of Children, Families and Social Issues, Birkbeck, University of London 2006, chapters 3 and 4.

86   Liz Hoggarth et al, Dudley Sure Start programmes – Evaluation of family support services, De Montfort University, 2006. See also Fiona Williams and Harriet Churchill, Empowering Parents in Sure Start Local, p 34.

87   New Deal for Communities: A Synthesis of New Programme Wide Evidence: 2006-07, NDC National Evaluation Phase 2, Research Report 39, DCLG, 2008; Rebecca Tunstall and Alice Coulter, Twenty five years on twenty estates; turning the tide?, JRF 2006.

88   New Deal for Communities: A Synthesis of New Programme Wide Evidence: 2006-07, p, 6; also national housing survey?

89   Over thirty local authority Trailblazer projects have been awards up to £260, 000 to develop holistic housing advice linked to employment services and advice ('More councils to offer homes and job advice', DCLG press release, Thursday, November 20th, 2008).

90   'Job advisors in Children's Centres to help parents into work', DWP press release, Thursday, 23rd October, 2008.

91   Peter Kemp, 'Housing Benefit and public housing in England', The future of public housing, Shelter, 2008, p 61.

92   DWP (2006) A new deal for welfare: empowering people to work. London: DWP

93   'First buyers benefitting from new shared equity scheme', DCLD press release, Wednesday, March 18th, 2009.

94   In January 2009 the government announced that it would extend a mortgage rescue scheme that has some of the features of the policy I an arguing for i.e. that homeowners in distress will be able to apply to their local authority to either sell part or all of their home to a local Housing Association, whilst retaining the right to stay in the home ('Mortgage rescue scheme extended

across England', DCLG press release, Friday, January 16th, 2009). Yet it is in fact a very tightly circumscribed and narrowly targeted scheme, only available to those who would be entitled to be re-housed under homelessness legislation. It thus does little in practical terms and nothing to create the sense of political legitimacy that could come with a far more universalist approach to housing provision and assistance.

95 Emily Silverman, Ruth Lupton, Alex Fenton, Attracting and retaining families in new urban mixed income communities, JRF, 2006, pp, 46,47.

96 Ibid, p 49.

97 For a full account of SAVE and New Earswick see Martin and Watkinson, Rebalancing communities Introducing mixed incomes into existing rented housing estates

98 Martin and Watkinson, Rebalancing communities Introducing mixed incomes into existing rented housing estates, p 7.

99 Rick Groves, Alan Middleton, Alan Murie and Kevin Broughton, Neighbourhoods that work: a study of the Bournville Estate, JRF, 2003.

100 Ibid, p 17.

101 Summary, Neighbourhoods that work, JRF, 2003.

Discussion Guide: In the Mix

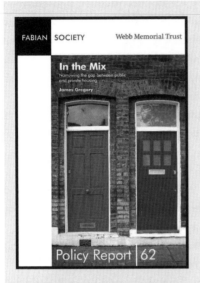

Changing lives by changing housing

'In the Mix: Narrowing the gap between public and private housing' by James Gregory

---

How to use this Discussion Guide

The guide can be used in various ways by Fabian Local Societies, local political party meetings and trade union branches, student societies, NGOs and other groups.

- You might hold a discussion among local members or invite a guest speaker – for example, an MP, academic or local practitioner to lead a group discussion.

- Four different key themes are suggested. You might choose to spend 15 – 20 minutes on each area, or decide to focus the whole discussion on one of the issues for a more detailed discussion.

A discussion could address some or all of the following questions:

1. Labour and housing

■ Why did the Labour Party fail to form an adequate counter-narrative to the ideology of right to buy in the 1980s?

2. The idea of assisted ownership

■ What should the left say about assisted home ownership as a means of greater asset equality?

■ How could we pursue assisted ownership without undermining the value of public housing?

3. Living in public housing

■ What active and innovative approaches could housing providers pursue to help break the link between public housing and worklessness?

■ What should the role of modern housing management encompass?

The Fabian Review, 2008

What can we learn from Obama's victory?

How can a party in office for more than a decade recapture its idealism? Can Labour hope to draw on the same popular enthusiasm that swept Barack Obama to victory?

In 'The Change We Need', edited by Nick Anstead and Will Straw, staffers from the Obama campaign come together with senior British and American politicians, academics, thinkers and campaigners to draw forwardlooking and optimistic lessons for the British progressive left.

Together they show that the opportunity can only be seized if we fundamentally rethink the ways we do politics in Britain, by rejecting the command-and-control model of the New Labour era and energising grassroots supporters.

British Muslims and the politics of fairness

In 'Fairness not Favours', Sadiq Khan MP argues that an effective agenda to provide opportunity and tackle extremism across all communities must go beyond a narrow approach to security, and sets out new proposals for a progressive agenda on inequality and life chances, public engagement in foreign policy, an inclusive Britishness, and rethinking the role of faith in public life.

The pamphlet puts the case for an effective agenda to provide opportunity and tackle extremism across all communities must go beyond a narrow approach to security, and sets out new proposals for a progressive agenda on inequality and life chances, public engagement in foreign policy, an inclusive Britishness, and rethinking the role of faith in public life.

Special offer: join the Fabians for just £9.95 and get this book free.

> 'The Fabians ask the most difficult questions, pushing Labour to make a bold, progressive case on taxation and the abolition of child poverty.' – **Polly Toynbee**

How can we make poverty history at home?

One in five children still grows up in poverty in Britain. Yet all the political parties now claim to care about 'social justice'. This report sets a litmus test by which Brown, Cameron and Campbell must be judged.

'Narrowing the Gap' is the final report of the Fabian Commission on Life Chances and Child Poverty, chaired by Lord Victor Adebowale. The Fabian Society is the only think tank with members. Join us and help us put poverty and equality at the centre of the political agenda.

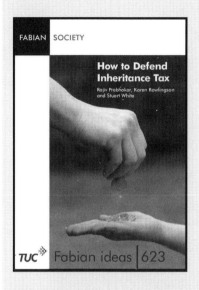

How to defend inheritance tax

Inheritance tax is under attack, and not just from the political right. The critics of this tax have dominated the debate over recent years but, as the authors of 'How to Defend Inheritance Tax' argue, this tax is one of the best tools we have for tackling inequality and kick starting Britain's stalled social mobility.

Defending inheritance tax is not just the responsibility of politicians – there must be a citizen-led campaign too. In this Fabian Ideas pamphlet, **Rajiv Prabhakar, Karen Rowlingson and Stuart White** provide progressives with the tools they need to win this argument.

They set out the evidence on inheritance and inequality, tackle the common objections to the tax, and demonstrate the moral and pragmatic arguments for an inheritance tax.

JOIN THE FABIANS TODAY
Join us and receive two Fabian Reviews, plus our acclaimed Fabian Special: 'The Change We Need: What Britain can learn from Obama's victory'

I'd like to become a Fabian for just £9.95

I understand that should at any time during my six-month introductory membership period I wish to cancel, I will receive a refund and keep all publications received without obligation. After six months I understand my membership will revert to the annual rate as published in *Fabian Review*, currently £33 (ordinary) or £16 (unwaged).

Name	Date of birth
Address	
	Postcode
Email	
Telephone	

Instruction to Bank   Originator's ID: 971666

Bank/building society name	DIRECT Debit
Address	
	Postcode
Acct holder(s)	
Acct no.	Sort code

I instruct you to pay direct debits from my account at the request of the Fabian Society. The instruction is subject to the safeguards of the Direct Debit Guarantee.

Signature	Date

Return to:
Fabian Society Membership
FREEPOST SW 1570
11 Dartmouth Street
London
SW1H 9BN